P9-DFL-987

Diagonal (or On-Point) Set

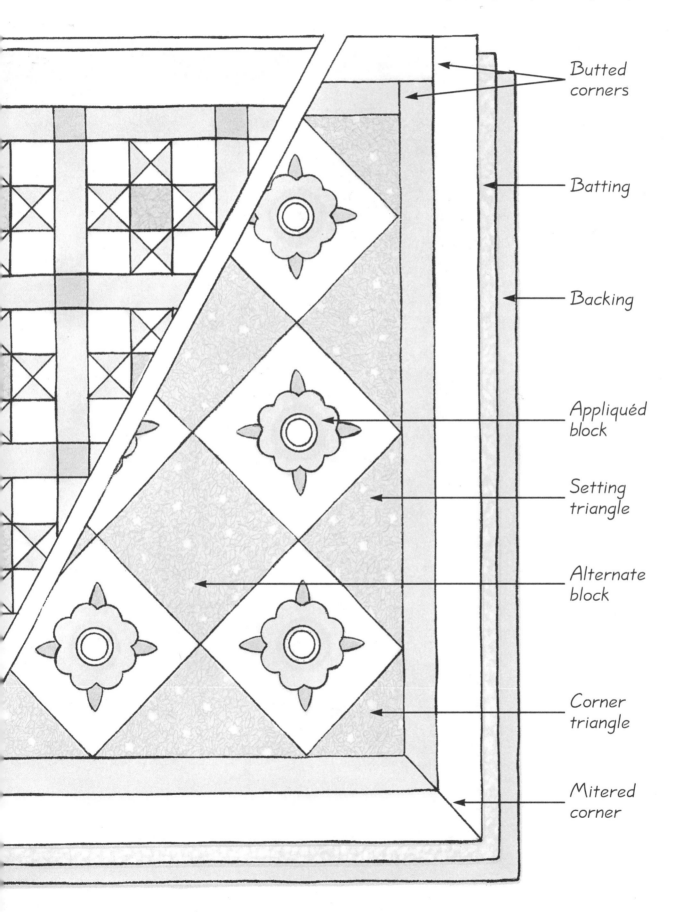

Butted corners

Batting

Backing

Appliquéd block

Setting triangle

Alternate block

Corner triangle

Mitered corner

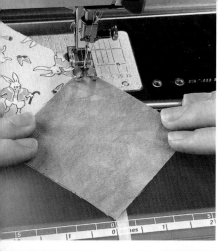

Rodale's Successful
Quilting Library®

Best
All-Time
Tips for
Quilters

Ellen Pahl, Editor

Rodale Press, Inc.
Emmaus, Pennsylvania

OUR PURPOSE

"We inspire and enable people to improve their lives and the world around them."

© 1999 by Rodale Press, Inc.

All rights reserved. No part of this publication may be reproduced or transmitted in any form or by any means, electronic or mechanical, including photocopy, recording, or any other information storage and retrieval system, without the written permission of the publisher.

The writers and editors who compiled this book have tried to make all of the contents as accurate and as correct as possible. Illustrations, photographs, and text have all been carefully checked and cross-checked. However, due to the variability of personal skill, tools, materials, and so on, neither the writers nor Rodale Press, Inc., assumes any responsibility for any injuries suffered or for damages or other losses incurred that result from the material presented herein. All instructions should be carefully studied and clearly understood before beginning any project.

Printed in the United States of America on acid-free ∞ , recycled ♻ paper

Editor: Ellen Pahl
Contributing Editor: Jane Townswick
Writers: Jane Hall, Dixie Haywood, Cyndi Hershey, Gail Kessler, Nancy O'Bryant Puentes, Susan Stein, Janet Wickell, and Darra Williamson
Series Designer: Sue Gettlin
Book Designers: Sandy Freeman and Chris Rhoads
Layout Designer: Keith Biery
Illustrator: Mario Ferro
Interior and Cover Photographer: Mitch Mandel
Interior Photographer (editor photo on page 7): Kurt Wilson
Photo Direction and Stylist: Sandy Freeman
Photography Editor: James A. Gallucci
Photo on page 103: Courtesy of American Quilter's Society; photographer Charles R. Lynch
Models: Erana Bumbardatore and Ellen Pahl
Copy Editor: Erana Bumbardatore
Manufacturing Coordinator: Patrick T. Smith
Indexer: Nan Badgett
Editorial Assistance: Sue Nickol

On the cover: Summertime by Dixie Haywood, Pensacola, Florida

On this page: Oak and Sumac by Dixie Haywood, Pensacola, Florida

Rodale Home and Garden Books
Vice President and Editorial Director: Margaret J. Lydic
Managing Editor, Rodale Quilt Books: Suzanne Nelson
Director of Design and Production: Michael Ward
Associate Art Director: Carol Angstadt
Production Manager: Robert V. Anderson Jr.
Studio Manager: Leslie M. Keefe
Copy Director: Dolores Plikaitis
Manufacturing Manager: Mark Krahforst
Office Manager: Karen Earl-Braymer

We're always happy to hear from you.

For questions or comments concerning the editorial content of this book, please write to:

Rodale Press, Inc.
Book Readers' Service
33 East Minor Street
Emmaus, PA 18098

Look for other Rodale books wherever books are sold. Or call us at (800) 848-4735.

For more information about Rodale Press and the books and magazines we publish, visit our World Wide Web site at:
http://www.rodalepress.com

Library of Congress Cataloging-in-Publication Data published the first volume of this series as:

Rodale's successful quilting library.
    p. cm.
Includes index.
ISBN 0–87596–760–4 (hc: v. 1:alk paper)
1. Quilting. 2. Patchwork. I. Soltys, Karen Costello. II. Rodale Press.
TT835.R622 1997
746.46'041—dc21   96–51316

Best All-Time Tips for Quilters:
ISBN 0–87596–822–8

Distributed in the book trade
by St. Martin's Press

2 4 6 8 10 9 7 5   hardcover

Contents

Introduction

I've come a long way since the first quilt I made when I was in college in the early 1970s. My grandmother Elizabeth Ross had been a quilter, but she lived 1,200 miles away, and regretfully, I did *not* learn quilting from her. I simply inherited her love of small bits of fabric sewn together to make one beautiful whole. So when I plunged in to make a quilt, I did just about everything wrong. I made paper patterns with ⅝-inch seam allowances and I pinned them to the fabric, just as I did in dressmaking. I used polyester fabrics, denim from my jeans, some cottons from my school dresses, and thin, gauzy scraps left over from making peasant blouses. I didn't even use batting—I used a flannel sheet between the layers, and I tied them together with pearl cotton and square knots. I sure could have used some tips!

One thing I've discovered since that first quilt is that quilters are a wonderful group. They are very supportive, and they love to share information and secrets for success. That's one reason why we decided to put together this volume of *Best All-Time Tips for Quilters*. We went to some of the best quilters and quilting teachers in the country, and we asked them for their most valuable insights. These are authors, teachers, award-winning quilters, and quilt-show judges. In this book, you have the best wisdom from at least a dozen top-notch quiltmakers.

We've covered everything, from soup to nuts. This book is perfect for dipping into a little bit at a time. There's a chapter on planning, to get you off to a good start. Then move on to chapters on color and fabric. Check out the tools and gadgets that the Rodale quilt book editors like in "Quilter's Lifesavers." Read tips on making the most of your sewing space. Save time with piecing shortcuts, easy quilting designs, pressing pointers, and time-shavers. Learn how to clean, care for, and display your quilts. Avoid aches and pains, and get the most out of your travel time. Check out the chapter on quilt shows before you attend one, or if you dream of entering one of your quilts.

There's a wealth of information here, whether you're a novice quilter or one who's been around the block. Our team of writers consisted of Jane Hall, Dixie Haywood, Cyndi Hershey, Gail Kessler, Nancy O'Bryant Puentes, Susan Stein, Janet Wickell, and Darra Williamson. Among the others who provided expert tips were Karen Kay Buckley, Sharyn Craig, Mimi Dietrich, and Mary Stori. As usual, I learned an incredible amount in the process of editing this book and making many of the samples. I tried lots of new products and techniques that make quilting easier or more trouble-free. The props and samples I accumulated for this book filled up an entire office (in addition to my own office), and I made lots of new quilting friends.

I even learned how much silk fabric there is in a man's necktie and how to stabilize it for stitching!

Well, like I said, I've come a long way. My old quilt is now quite laughable, but it keeps me grounded and reminds me that there are always beginners out there who need good information. That's the driving force behind this series. We give you clear, concise instructions with detailed photographs to accompany the text every step of the way, so you're guaranteed success in all your quilting endeavors. I hope you enjoy putting these tips to use.

Ellen Pahl

Ellen Pahl
Editor

Planning
Pays Off

R emember the saying, "There's more than one way to skin a cat?" Well, that applies to quilting, too. There are a myriad of ways to plan and make a quilt. Some people like to jump right in and just let a quilt happen. Others plan it all out, right down to the binding. According to Susan Stein, quilting teacher and designer, no one way is right or wrong. Whatever works for you is right. Usually a little advance planning does help, even if it's simply getting to the fabric store to add to your stash. Then when inspiration strikes at 11:30 at night, at least you'll be prepared!

Getting Started

Occasionally a quilt design pops into your head and you can go to your stash and begin cutting and sewing without any preparation. More often, though, you need to spend time up front deciding what you want the design to look like. Consider the mood you're trying to create, what the end use of the quilt will be (wallhanging, bed quilt, and so on), and the room where it will be used.

Next you'll need to figure yardages, colors, and value placement. You should evaluate your stash and determine what fabrics you may need to buy, and then come up with a game plan. The trick is to be able to audition different ideas and do some trial runs without cutting up lots of excess fabric. And you don't want to waste time that could be better spent at the sewing machine. The tools presented here range from simple and low-tech all the way to high-tech computer software. Pick the ones that appeal to you to pave the way from a successful design to a beautiful finished quilt.

On with the Plan

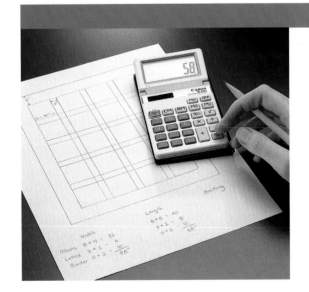

Quick Yardage Estimate

When making a quilt with a repeat block, you don't need to graph out the entire design to figure the yardage. Do a rough sketch, and multiply the number of blocks across the length and width of the quilt by their finished size to determine the size of the quilt. Multiply the number of lattice strips by their finished width, and add that number to the block totals to determine the border lengths needed. **To get a rough estimate of the fabric needed, determine the yardage for the back of the quilt, add 25 to 50 percent more for seam allowances, and divide the total proportionally among the number of fabrics you are going to use.**

Planning on Graph Paper

Tip

A pencil-point eraser with a brush on the end makes it easy to change lines without erasing ones you want to keep.

Draw your quilt design on graph paper. Paper with ⅛-inch squares works better for quilts than paper with ¼-inch squares. You can assign one square per inch and simply count the squares to get the dimensions of the final quilt when your design is finished. If your computer has the capability to print graph paper, you don't even have to purchase a whole pad but can print sheets as you need them, instead.

Audition Borders

Audition borders by laying tracing paper over the block and lattice layout and sketching different pieced or appliquéd borders. This is especially useful for round-robin quilts, where different quilters plan the successive borders that surround the center block. When it's your turn to add a border, take a photo of the quilt top when you receive it and then paste the photo onto a sheet of graph paper. Use the tracing paper overlay to try different border treatments. Or you can simply draw the quilt as it appears onto the graph paper yourself.

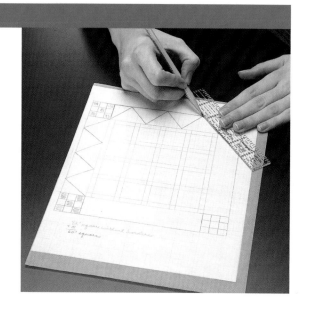

Color Schemes

After you get your design graphed out, you may want to try different color schemes. **Lay tracing paper over your graph paper pattern, and try out different ideas for color and value placement.** If you enjoy this process, make it a goal to show how various color plans can completely change the visual impact of a quilt. Start a notebook of the pages you draw, for future reference and to teach others (who may be less patient with colored pencils!) what you've discovered.

Specialty Graph Papers

If you are using triangles, diamonds, or hexagons as part of a block or in an overall pattern, there is graph paper available that makes the job of drawing out a one-patch design much easier. For diamond or triangle elements within a whole design, like a sampler, cut pieces from specialized graph paper and use a glue stick to paste them into the appropriate places on regular graph paper.

Using the Copy Machine

Use the copy machine to make multiple copies of your block pattern, and then cut and paste the blocks to make different arrangements for the quilt top. Rotate blocks, add lattice, use alternate plain blocks with your appliqué or pieced blocks, try out a pieced lattice or a pieced alternate block, and try anything else you can imagine. Feel free to play and be creative.

Color Away

After you decide on an arrangement, copy it several times and color the copies in different color schemes. If you have plenty of the fabrics you are planning to use, cut small swatches of fabric and glue them to the photocopies. Put the designs on the wall, and stand back from them to get the overall effect.

PLANNING PAYS OFF

Copy Your Fabric

If you are short of the fabrics that you plan to use, **color photocopy your fabric. Make several color copies of the fabrics and then cut out pieces, without seam allowances, for the block. Using repositionable or removable tape, tape the pieces into blocks.** New dispensers are available that lay a strip of tape on the back of a piece of paper simply by running the dispenser across the paper. Or use a glue stick with a weak adhesive similar to the glue on Post-it Notes. Audition different arrangements of the pieces until you find the best one.

Planning a Quilt from a Favorite Fabric

Tip

Leave plenty of space between windows. Closely spaced openings may give you a distorted preview, since more of the print will be visible at one time.

Fabrics you love on the bolt sometimes lose their appeal when they're cut into small pieces for patchwork. Check before you cut by making a fabric viewer. Using lightweight cardboard or a manila folder, cut openings in a range of patch sizes you normally use. Position the windowed cardboard against a piece of fabric, and move it around to preview how pieces will look when cut from different areas. **If you have a specific block in mind, make the windows match the actual finished sizes and shapes of the patches.** Take the viewer with you when you shop for fabric.

Off-the-Wall Planning

Tip

Try using Triangle Paper by Quiltime. It fits well onto fat quarters and makes the sewing of triangle-squares very accurate and easy.

Try planning your next quilt as you go. Start with basic, easy-to-assemble units such as half-square triangles. Use a bundle of hand-dyed fabrics and a favorite print to sew a few dozen squares. Play with them on a design wall. When you run out of fabric or get tired of making squares, sew some blocks together. Arrange the blocks on the wall. Do they need lattice to separate them, or plain blocks to make a larger quilt? At this point, you will see what your quilt will look like. Sometimes it's more fun to plunge in and start sewing. "Listen" to your fabrics rather than planning and figuring first.

The Quilter's
Problem Solver

Designing on a Computer

If you are designing a quilt with repeating patterns, the computer is a wonderful tool. As more and more people use computers at home and work, computers become less intimidating. A good program will allow you to draw your own block or choose one from a broad array of traditional choices, color it, add fabric patterns, and place it into a quilt layout. The blocks can then be rotated, and the lattice and borders can be manipulated to any size and configuration. When the design is complete, the computer should be able to print out the quilt diagram, with shading and fabric patterns, and it should figure the yardages for you.

There are several computer programs designed especially for quilters: Electric Quilt, Block-Base, and Quilt-Pro are three popular ones. There are also general-use design programs, like Corel Draw, that can be adapted to quilting. Which program you choose will depend on the type and capabilities of your computer, and on how comfortable you are using a computer. Ask friends and computer dealers which program best suits your needs.

One very exciting feature you may want is the ability to scan actual fabric into the computer to use in your design. You may also want to print quilt labels and original fabric. If you plan to foundation-piece your quilt, you can print out the pattern sheets on your computer and make them any size you wish. There are even programs available with hundreds of designs all ready to go.

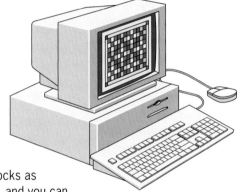

BlockBase allows you to review 3,500 quilt blocks as if you were looking at a slide show, all in color, and you can stop the program at any time to learn the origin of the block, print out a copy, or fill it in with different patterns and colors.

If you are undecided on whether to purchase a computer program or not, decide on the type of quilt you make the most. If it has a repeating design with lattice and borders, and it utilizes a limited number of fabrics, a computer program will help you figure out a plan, calculate yardage, and show where colors will work the best. If you most often make quilts without blocks and you like to play directly with the fabrics when deciding placement, the computer will not help.

If you are a quilting teacher who likes to use handouts, the computer makes very professional-looking ones and can be used to show students different options for settings and sizes of projects. A distinct disadvantage to buying a computer program is that you may become so addicted to playing with it that you never get to the sewing machine. Other than some printouts, you will have nothing to show for your time, and paper will not keep you warm or decorate your walls!

PLANNING PAYS OFF

Color Cookbook
for Quilters

J ust as the right blend of spices can add zest to any recipe, a perfect combination of colors and fabrics can create quilts that radiate a variety of wonderful flavors, from familiar and fun to exquisite and exotic. Gail Kessler, former owner of The Summer House Needleworks quilt shop, is a master "color chef" who shows you how to stir together great fabric ingredients and cook up some fantastic quilts.

Get Cooking

There is an infinite world of wonderful color and fabric combinations available to anyone who enjoys making quilts. Arriving at the color palettes you love most is a creative journey that lets you continue developing your individual color preferences with each quilt you make.

In this chapter there are 10 innovative tips for thinking about color and how to blend fabrics together in many different "recipes" to create quilts that sparkle with flavor and vitality. Use these themes as jumping-off points to get your imagination simmering. Then go to your stash and pull as many fabrics as possible—the more the better is my theory. Don't be afraid to experiment and improvise. You may just come up with a favorite recipe of your own.

Some of the blocks and fabrics, plus many other pieced and appliquéd blocks, are available by mail as Block-of-the-Month kits from The Summer House Needleworks in Oley, Pennsylvania. For more information, see "Quilter's Marketplace" on page 124.

The Recipes

All-American

As fun as a Fourth of July picnic—combine scraps of red, white, and blue to create a real family treasure. **It's okay to mix in some cream-color fabrics with the whites to give your quilt more homespun charm, as in this group of four Kansas Troubles blocks.** For scrap quilts in this theme, take three paper bags and fill each bag with scraps of one color. Then reach into each bag (with eyes closed), and pull out one red, one white, and one blue fabric. Use these fabrics for your block to achieve a truly scrappy effect.

Home Baked

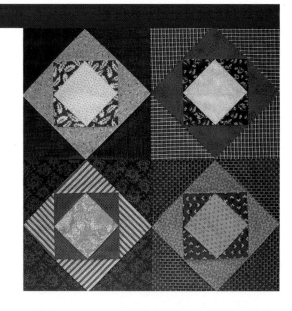

Chocolate, cinnamon, saffron noodles, candy apples, and gingerbread—combine these colors for a cozy, hearth-and-home scrappy look that any country soul would love. Here we've combined four Square-in-a-Square blocks to create a warm, homemade flavor.

Tip

You don't need to perfectly match the colors in every quilt. Just keep the overall "flavor" of the fabrics similar, and your eyes will blend them for you.

Country French

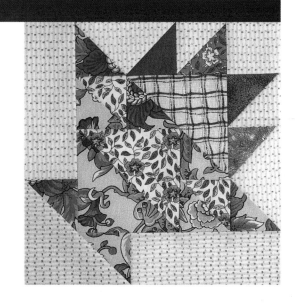

It's fun to collect bright, sunny yellow fabrics and pair them with brilliant royal blues. Be sure to mix large prints with small to achieve a real Provençal look, as in this May Basket block. Some of the prints can be both yellow and blue, and can contain traces of green, red, or even black. This is a fun combination of colors to try, especially if you haven't used much bright yellow in the past.

New Age Café

Here are the clean, sophisticated, and subtle colors of tea, cappuccino, and espresso served in dark teal cups. Additional "cream" changes the value of the neutrals. Arrange little piles of very light to medium rose fabrics (tea). Do the same with light tan to chocolate (cappuccino) and medium to dark walnut (espresso). It's fun to trail or step the color gradations in a Twisted Log Cabin, as shown.

From the Sea

Think of the beautiful turquoise or aqua of the tropical oceans; the striking colors of the dazzling, exotic, salt-water fish; bright yellow bananas; and coral-color mangoes accented with fresh, zesty lime. You've just created a festive tropical feast that can't help but make you smile as you sew! Here are four simple Square-in-a-Square blocks that will transport you to the tropics in no time flat.

Tip

The most simplistic piecing designs come alive with flavor when you use bright exotic colors like these!

Asian Flair

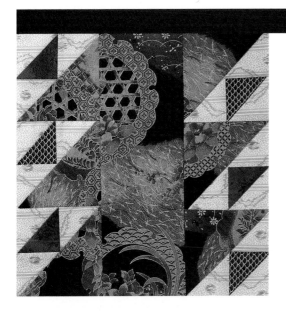

Elegant, swirling, Oriental-style fabrics have a special, formal look that's hard to resist. Capture the jewel-like colors from an extravagant larger print with smaller-scale fabrics. Geometric prints often balance and complement these fabrics, as in this Wampum block.

Country Gourmet

See what happens when you combine bright, rich color combinations and put them on a dull, warm, gray background. Use stripes or plaids to give your work a country flavor, and allow the brighter colors you use to cast a beautiful glow, as in this Odd Fellows Chain block.

COLOR COOKBOOK FOR QUILTERS

Take-Out Drive Through

Many of today's fabric companies plan coordinated fabric lines as collections to be used together in a quilt. Quilt shops and mail-order companies sometimes offer small cuts from each bolt in a collection as a collector or designer package. **This is a great opportunity to try a new "taste" in your quilts without investing a lot of time or trouble.**

Tip

You can always add a dash of fabric from your stash to give the quilt your special signature.

Southwestern Fiesta

Playing with a salsa theme, yellow, red, green, and black join forces for this spicy combination. The chili pepper print helps set the mood. The striped fabric adds movement. This color theme gives you an opportunity to play with fabrics other than florals. For a zippy substitution, use marbled fabrics in hot colors in place of the orange and green polka dot. This block is called Hobson's Kiss.

Pastel Dessert Mints

These sweet, melt-in-your-mouth colors combine with white to create a soft, refreshing touch in this Rambler block. The fabrics used here are printed to resemble hand-dyed yardage. The subtle variations in color add interest to the block.

Getting Out of a Color Rut

Problem	Solution

I'm in a rut. Every project I make seems to be using the same color palette.

❏ Cleanse your palette. Make a black-and-white block or small quilt. Concentrate on contrast, scale, pattern, and texture *without* color. Taking a break from making color decisions gets you out of your routine and makes you think about other important aspects of fabric design.

❏ Purchase a fabric collection or kit in colors you would never ordinarily use, and make a fun project as a special gift to yourself or a friend.

❏ Take your project-in-the-making to your favorite quilt shop and ask for help. Shop owners and their employees pick colors for a living—take advantage of their expertise!

❏ Go for a walk and look at nature. Look at the sunrise and sunset. Pick up a beautiful rock or seashell and study its colors. Walk up and down the produce aisle and make quilt salad! Inspiration is everywhere!

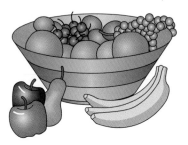

❏ Take a look at your collection. Perhaps your fabric stash needs refreshing. Ideally, you should have nearly equal amounts of each color (whether or not they are your favorite). You should also have about equal amounts of light, medium, and dark values of each color. Sort your fabrics by color, and make a shopping list of the colors and values you are missing.

Fabric Lover's
Guide to Life

Quilters love fabric! It is the one thing that all quilters have in common, regardless of the style of quilting they prefer. And it's not just the color, but the feel of fabric that appeals. Put a piece of fabric in front of a quilter and she has to touch it. In this chapter, Cyndi Hershey, teacher and quilt-shop owner, gives you the inside scoop on storing and using fabric. The more you know about your fabric, the more confident you will feel as you begin your next project. In fact, you may end up loving fabric even more!

Storing Fabrics

There are three basic rules for fabric storage: minimize prolonged exposure to direct light, avoid moisture, and maximize your storage space. Try to store fabric vertically as much as possible to best utilize your space. **Hang fabric from pants or skirt hangers, especially the "waterfall" types, which are very space efficient. Then hang the fabric in a closet out of direct light.** You can also pad the bar of a hanger with some pipe insulation to hang larger pieces or more delicate fabrics, such as silk or wool. Slit the pipe insulation with a utility knife, and slip it over the hanger.

Tip

If you don't have extra closet space, try balancing a piece of PVC pipe between two shelf units or suspending the pipe from the ceiling in a dead space in the room.

Fabric Shelves

Folding fabric and organizing it by color on open shelves allows your fabric to "breathe." **To protect the fabric from light, hang fabric drapes in front of each shelf unit** or place each stack of fabric in a cotton pillowcase. You can also purchase wire shelf-organizer systems that have slide-out baskets from home centers. These are a great way to keep your shelves or closets in order, and they provide easy access to fabrics.

Box It Up!

Many people prefer clear plastic boxes for their fabric storage. The main problem with these is that they tend to trap moisture. **If you use them, cut or drill holes in the lids or the sides of the boxes. You will be able to stack them for the best use of space.** Cardboard boxes, especially those that are all the same uniform size, such as file or banker's boxes, can also work. Simply line them with acid-free tissue paper or tinfoil to keep the acid in the cardboard away from your fabric.

FABRIC LOVER'S GUIDE TO LIFE

Large Amounts of Yardage

If you purchase yardage in large amounts for quilt backs or because you have a home business, you know how challenging it can be to store it. The more that you can roll—rather than fold—fabric, the better. **Rolling prevents fold lines (reducing ironing time), and it allows you to store *vertically* rather than horizontally.** This frees up shelf space to use for other things. Ask the store where you shop most frequently for a few empty bolt boards or fabric tubes. Most shop owners will be glad to give you some.

Bolts & Beyond

Another option for storing large amounts of yardage is to invest a few dollars in some PVC pipe, and have it cut to the lengths that you want. PVC is extremely sturdy, moisture resistant, and inexpensive. **The fabric may be rolled onto the tubes doubled in half like it was on the bolt, or opened up to its full width.** The rolls can be stored upright in a corner or a tall box that you cover with fabric or decorative paper. You can also make a suspension system by linking several lengths of pipe together with chain or rope and then hanging them from the ceiling like a giant waterfall hanger!

"I Can't Throw It Away!"

Storing "scraps" (and we'll use that term loosely!) can be a problem. They just seem to multiply. Again, you can divide them into fabric types and color groups and use plastic boxes as described in "Box It Up!" on page 21. Wicker baskets are also nice; they allow air circulation and look pretty on a shelf. **But the most space-efficient storage is to use hanging sweater or shoe bags. Fold and store scraps by color on the sweater "shelves." You can also fold or roll fabric and store it in the shoe pockets.** Shoe bags can be hung in a closet or on the *back* of a door. Once again, you're storing *vertically*.

Prewashing Fabric

Treat fabrics as gently as you will treat your finished quilt. Dumping fabric into the washer with hot water and harsh detergent and then throwing it into a hot dryer will fade and stress the fabric. Use Orvus quilt soap, a mild, phosphate-free soap used by textile museums and fabric lovers. Or try Quiltwash to remove overdyes, sizing, and residues. Wash fabrics *gently* in cool water with little or no soap. Test dark fabrics for color retention first by placing them in cool water. If there is color loss, treat with Retayne to set the dyes for up to 10 washes.

Tip

Orvus is thick and highly concentrated. Before adding it to the rest of the wash water, mix a small amount with water to dilute it.

Fighting Tangles, Wrinkles & Thread Balls

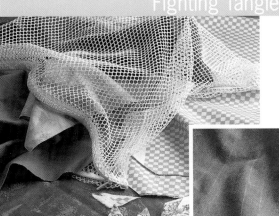

Always open your fabric completely before placing in the washer. **Any fold is likely to develop an abrasion line during the wash. To help prevent raveling and tangles, cut a *small* triangle off all four corners of the fabric before washing. Wash small pieces or scraps by placing them in a mesh laundry bag.** Or it may be just as easy to place them in a sink, swish them around, and then hang or lay them flat to dry. Remember to be gentle, and use low agitation!

Tip

For kits or blocks-of-the month, rinse the small fabric pieces in the sink, blot them between the layers of a towel, and iron them dry.

Things to Do When Pressing & Folding Fabric

Expanding Your Ironing Board

When pressing large pieces of fabric, a traditional ironing board can seem too small for the job. The larger the pressing surface, the easier and faster this job will be. You can purchase a commercially available item called a **Big Board, which is made to fit on top of your present ironing board. This gives you a large rectangular surface that is more conducive to pressing 45-inch widths of fabric** because it eliminates the narrow end of your ironing board.

FABRIC LOVER'S GUIDE TO LIFE

More "Pressing" Thoughts

To make a temporary large pressing surface, you can **pad the surface of your cutting or sewing table with commercial felt table padding or even several thick terry towels. Silver heat-reflective fabric is available at most fabric shops and may be placed over the padding,** if desired. When you're finished pressing, it is easy to roll up the entire thing and store it until the next time.

Getting a Grip

When pressing smaller pieces of fabric or even small portions of your quilt, it is helpful to pad and stabilize the pressing surface. Purchase a yard each of black and white heavy, double-napped flannel. Open them both up to a single layer, place them together, and then fold both in half together. Lay this on top of your ironing board. **When pressing light fabrics, place them on the white flannel, and when pressing dark fabrics, place them on the black flannel to prevent lint transfer.** The flannel will grip and hold your fabric in place, help to eliminate crease marks from previous seams, and make "shiny" spots a thing of the past.

Folding Your Fabric for Storage

Fold your fabric in half with opposite selvages together, as it was on the bolt. The fabric is now ready to rotary cut without refolding. Fold it as often as necessary to fit onto your shelf or into your container, but try not to fold it any more than needed. Tag your fabric after it is washed, pressed, and folded. On a small card or piece of paper, write the amount of yardage and indicate when it was washed and pressed. **Attach your notes to the fabric with a basting gun.** Then you will never have to wonder if you already prepared the fabric for use.

Fabric Collections

Everyone has color preferences, and they become quite obvious when you look at a quilter's fabric stash! **Every so often, you should take a fabric inventory and see where things stand.** Most quilters will find that they are heavy on several colors and more than lacking in others. Be objective with your review, and the next time you go to the store, try to buy fabrics to round out your palette, instead of just buying fabrics for a specific project.

Tip

Don't forget to check your inventory for a range of values (lights and darks), not just colors!

Start a File System

Maintaining an inventory or catalog system for your fabric collection may be extremely helpful. **Keep track of each piece of fabric that you purchase by recording the following information: fiber content, width, manufacturer, original yardage amount purchased, store where purchased, and date of purchase.** Most importantly, attach a swatch of the fabric. Keep this information on index cards in a file box or even in a recipe file notebook with plastic sleeves. Now you have an excellent reference when shopping for additional fabrics or in case you need to find more of a particular favorite.

Tip

Make a note on the cards or fabric tags as you use some or all of the fabric and adjust the remaining yardage.

Feeding Your Stash

If you can begin to think of fabric as your crayons or paint palette, it will change the way that you buy fabrics in the future. Instead of buying for a particular project, concentrate on buying different styles as well as different colors of fabric. **Do you tend to lean toward florals and then find that you can't use more than a few in one project? Then perhaps you need to buy some plaids, checks, or random prints for balance.** Do you love novelty prints but then wonder how to use them? Try adding some small-scale or monotone prints to showcase the novelties.

Tip

Most quilters are lacking interesting "lights" in their stash. Lights are usually backgrounds and are used proportionately more than most other fabrics!

FABRIC LOVER'S GUIDE TO LIFE

25

A Hollywood Shopping Strategy

Think of fabrics as actors in a movie or stage production. **One or two actors are billed as the stars, and the others are supporting actors. And there is usually a walk-on with a very limited part.** He or she may be the one you remember most due to a funny line or dramatic performance. Fabrics in a quilt work in much the same way. You'll need the star, a main or theme print, and several supporting fabrics. The walk-on is a bright or unusual accent fabric used in a smaller quantity—it may make the difference between a so-so quilt and a truly remarkable accomplishment.

Tip

Not everyone can be the "star" in a production, and not every fabric can play that role in a quilt. Don't neglect to find supporting actors.

Changing Your Perspective

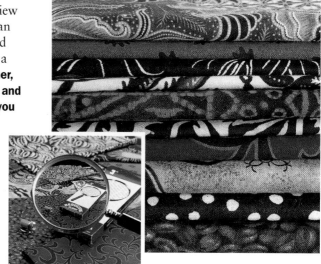

When shopping for fabric, you view it from a different perspective than you will when it's in your finished quilt. When choosing fabrics for a single project, **stack them together, step back at least 10 to 15 feet, and view them from the side so that you only see the narrow edges.** This way you get a better feel for how they will work *together* in the quilt. **Another trick is to use a reducing glass to view fabric.** It allows you to view the fabric as though you are much further away and gives you a more accurate idea of how the fabric will look in your project.

Tip

Purchase a reducing glass at a quilt shop or art supply store. Or you can buy a door peephole at a hardware store.

How Much Should I Buy?

When you're buying fabric for your stash, follow one of these guidelines. **If it's a fabric that you love and feel could be a main print or border of a bed quilt, buy 3 to 4 yards.** This will give you enough in length for borders of a queen- to king-size quilt and some extra across the width for piecing or appliqué. **If you think it will make a perfect secondary print or a blender fabric, buy 1 to 2 yards. If it would be a great accent, buy ½ to 1 yard.** Always buy plenty; you never know if you will be able to find it again!

Oh, no! I've run out of fabric!

Don't fret! This happens to plenty of quilters!

Step one is to try to get more at the store from which you purchased it initially. Realize, though, that they may no longer have it. Most fabrics have a fairly short life span, and even if the shop owner is willing to order it again, it may not be possible for her to get it.

Step two is to try other stores. Cut out a 2-inch square of your fabric and keep it in your purse. That way, you'll be ready in case you stumble upon an unexpected fabric or quilt shop. Pin it to a large yellow self-stick note, along with the amount of yardage you need. Also, ask your quilting friends or guild members if they have it in their stash and would be willing to sell you some.

If this approach fails, try to remain calm! You can continue your search on the Internet, if you're so inclined. There is a web site for finding missing fabrics (www.knoxgroup.com/missingfabrics/). But why don't you try the approach of quilters throughout history: Make do! Sometimes your quilt will be more interesting in the long run because of it. Make it a creative opportunity.

Think about the role that the fabric plays in your quilt. This will help determine your choice of solutions.

Always cut everything first before you start piecing. Then if you have to change plans, it will be easier and you'll know before you sew!

Problem	Solutions and Other Make-Do Tactics
Ran out of border fabric.	Try using cornerstones, or even create a pieced border incorporating several different fabrics along with your original one.  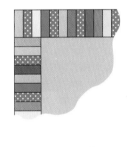 Design corner squares for an outer border that includes small pieces of the fabric. Put one piece of it into a patchwork unit like half- or quarter-square triangles, and sprinkle those throughout the border. Look for the same color combination, but in a different print. The substitute fabric can mimic the feel enough to keep a sense of continuity from the interior of the quilt to the border.
Ran out of background or any other fabric.	Try converting to the scrap quilt idea. Using multiple fabrics in similar color families will generally be the easiest and least stressful solution. You may be surprised at how much more interesting the quilt actually looks! Make one oddball block. Put it in the center intentionally. Piece the scraps to make a poverty patch or two—gather your leftover bits and stitch them together to make a larger, usable piece of fabric. Appliqué very small pieces of the fabric onto some larger pieces; use these as small centers on larger flowers, wings on birds, and so on. Piece together several different fabrics to create a random, colorful binding, and include small pieces of the fabric, to carry it as far as possible throughout the quilt.

Quilter's
Lifesavers

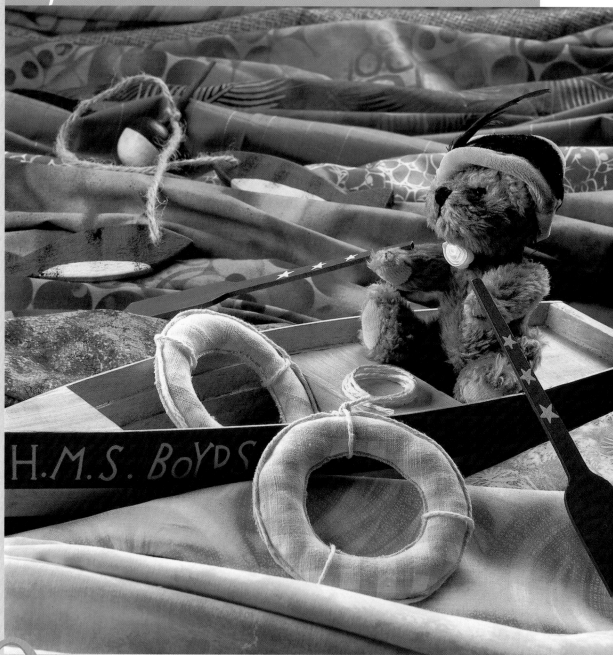

H.M.S. BOYDS

Quilting is exciting—new tools and gadgets are being developed all the time to help make things easier, quicker, or more efficient. Rodale Quilt Book editors regularly attend shows and scout for new products. Over the years, we've all developed and grown as quilters, adapting to new tools and techniques, picking those that we like best. Here we share a few of our *favorite things*, what we call *Quilter's Lifesavers*, most of which are available at your local quilt shop.

Editors' Favorites

Taming the Sliding Ruler

If you have ever had difficulty keeping your ruler from sliding while you cut, here's a nifty solution from Sally Schneider. **Place a needle grabber, a circle of rubber normally used to pull a stubborn needle through several layers of fabric, between the ruler and the fabric.** Put one on each end of the fabric, then place the ruler on top. The ruler will stay put and won't slip. Needle grabbers are inexpensive, reusable forever, easy to find, and simple to use. And they don't obscure your view of lines because you can place them away from important measurements.

Make your needle grabbers go even further by cutting them in half. Use one half on each end of the fabric.

Help for Sore Fingertips

Using your fingertip to guide a quilting needle back up through the layers of a quilt can produce calluses, or even bleeding, after a long period spent hand quilting. **Among the many different hand-quilting tools now available, Jane Townswick's very favorite is T.J.'s Quick Quilter.** Its bent handle makes it very comfortable to hold in the hand underneath a quilt, and the flat, smooth ridge along the top of the "spoon" makes it simple to angle a needle tip back up through the backing, batting, and quilt top.

Tip

Hold the T.J.'s Quick Quilter with the hand beneath the quilt in whatever way feels comfortable for you.

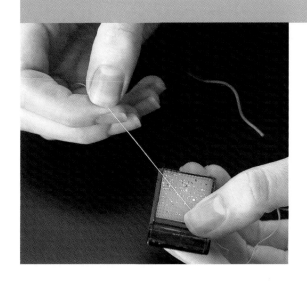

My Thread's in Heaven

With the stress that comes from being pulled in and out of fabric repeatedly during hand piecing, appliqué, or quilting, it's no wonder that kinks, tangles, fraying, and knots occur even in the finest threads. Jane Townswick loves a product that conditions thread so it will slide through fabric like butter, with hardly any wear and tear. **Simply run a strand of thread over the surface of Thread Heaven conditioner to coat it with a silky-smooth layer of silicone, and then watch snarls and tangles melt away!**

QUILTER'S LIFESAVERS

The Scissor Spot

Tip

A similar product is the Pin Place, which will conveniently hold your pins as you remove them during piecing.

The Scissor Spot is a magnetic disc that sticks to your sewing machine with a suction cup. It holds scissors or other metal tools. Use it on any part of your machine where there is enough space for the cup. Sally Schneider tried it and found that the top of the machine was best—it didn't interfere with the on/off switches or feed dog dials, and it was both handy and visible. Sliding the thread clips sideways to retrieve them worked much better than trying to lift them up because the magnet is quite strong. Most computerized machines are sufficiently shielded so that you can use the Scissor Spot without worrying.

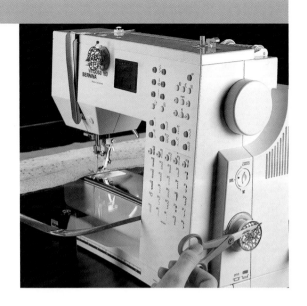

No-More-Pins Appliqué

Tip

This is a great method for Tahitian or Hawaiian appliqué with lots of narrow cut-out spaces.

How much more appliqué would you do if you didn't have to pin or baste tiny pieces into place? Here's a product that Sarah Dunn likes: **Roxanne's Glue-Baste-It, a water-soluble glue that comes with its own extra-narrow needle applicator. With this, you can apply tiny dabs of glue, one drop at a time, to temporarily baste even the tiniest or narrowest shape in place.** The glue holds firmly until you moisten the spot or wash the completed piece. If you've positioned it incorrectly, gently pull the two pieces apart and the glue will release. Then, just reglue the piece into place.

Basting Spray

Tip

Use basting spray to refresh a worn-out flannel design wall or hold appliqué shapes in place.

Fabric-friendly spray adhesives have taken the drudgery out of basting. Suzanne Nelson was able to turn this 44-inch-square quilt top into a nice, smooth quilt sandwich in 8 minutes flat. The resulting pin-free and tack-free surface is easy to machine quilt. Work in a well-ventilated area, always read the manufacturer's instructions, and spray on a surface that is easy to wipe down (the spray can settle on areas outside the quilt). Move your hand back and forth to get a light, even distribution of spray.

QUILTER'S LIFESAVERS

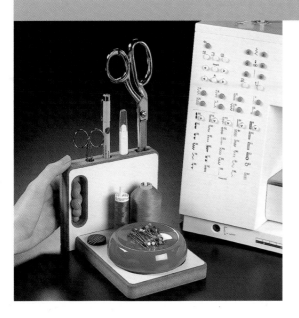

The VCR is ready, and your family is impatiently waiting while you round up sewing supplies for your handwork. Quilters often like to take advantage of movies to do quilting, binding, or appliqué. To minimize searching time, be sure to plan ahead for any opportunity by keeping supplies together. **Ellen Pahl discovered a wonderful product called the Grabbit Notions Nook. It holds all the essential supplies and can sit next to your sewing machine.** When you want to do some handwork in another room, just grab the portable accessory along with your project, and you'll never miss the beginning of a movie again.

Block Viewer

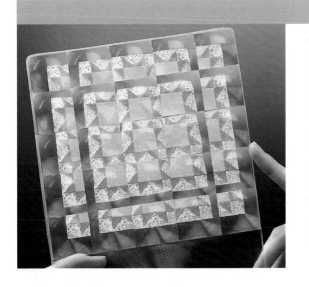

This handy gadget, the Multi-View Lens by Quilter's Rule, came to the rescue when Suzanne Nelson was planning a wedding quilt for her sister. **After making a test block in her chosen fabrics, Suzanne was able to preview multiple blocks through the viewer.** It's a quick-and-easy way to see what happens at block intersections after making just one block. With it, you'll be able to predict whether you want to set the blocks together or add lattice.

Tip

Use the viewer to get a sneak peak at how floor tile or ceramic tile will look in your home, too!

Sewing Extension Table

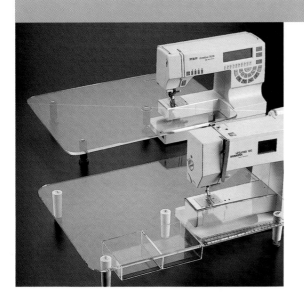

These sewing extension tables are truly lifesavers for machine quilting. After struggling through a baby quilt without a table, Ellen Pahl refuses to machine quilt without one. They give much-needed additional support and surface area for manipulating the bulk of a quilt. The surface is smooth and eliminates the drag of the quilt, enabling the quilter to have more control of both machine-guided and free-motion quilting. They're also great for general sewing and piecing, giving a two-level work surface. **The two types shown are the Sew Steady on the Pfaff and the Clutter Gutter on the Bernina.**

QUILTER'S LIFESAVERS

31

E very quilter dreams of a "room of her own," complete with a large, brightly lit design wall, custom-built tables for cutting and sewing, and endless storage for fabric and books. In the real world, however, many of us share sewing space with other family members, carving a tiny niche from the kitchen, family room, bedroom . . . or even hall closet. In this chapter, writer Darra Williamson says, "Don't let limited workspace limit you!" Check out her surefire tips for making efficient use of whatever space you have at hand.

Workspace Setup

Efficient Workstation Layout

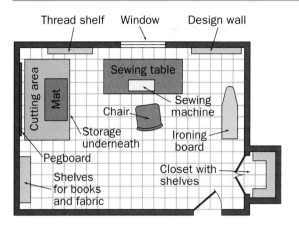

Thread shelf   Window   Design wall

Sewing table

Cutting area

Mat

Sewing machine

Chair

Storage underneath

Ironing board

Pegboard

Shelves for books and fabric

Closet with shelves

The most efficient layout for your workstation is a U formation. Keep your sewing machine, iron, cutting board, and design surface all within this compact area. Take advantage of every nook and cranny. Wall-mount a grid system, pegboard, or hanging pocket organizer for tools and notions. Place shelving above windows or doors. Explore home improvement stores and catalogs for stacking baskets, bins, and other storage solutions.

Tip

An office-style chair not only offers good back support, but also is adjustable in height and can glide you effortlessly from task to task.

A Portable Design Wall

If space is at a premium, here is a portable solution for creating a design wall. Purchase a two-yard length of white flannel or felt, and trim it to door width. Turn the top edge, and stitch a 4-inch-wide rod pocket. Insert a wooden dowel into the pocket, and **drape the dowel over the top of a door so the fabric surface faces your work area. The dowel's weight holds the "wall" in place, and the door behind stabilizes the surface.** When you are finished working for the day, remove the "wall" and roll it around the dowel for easy storage.

Tip

Pin a layer of tissue paper over your design surface to hold unsewn pieces securely in place before rolling up your design wall.

Creating a Pressing Station

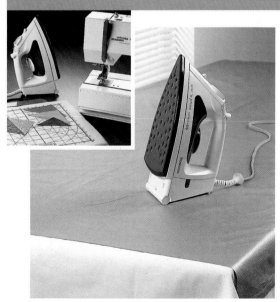

For convenience, maintain a small pressing station at your sewing machine. **Select a small pressing board that fits comfortably beside your machine and serves double duty by reversing to a cutting or sandpaper board.** If you don't have space *on top* of your surface, prop the pressing board over the nearest open drawer.

If possible, **create a separate pressing surface large enough for all your quilting needs. Cover a hollow door with two layers of cotton batting, and then muslin or silver heat-reflective fabric** (available at fabric stores). Position it over two file or storage cabinets, raising the height, if necessary, with wood blocks or bricks.

Tip

Store like items together. Notions, tools, and other gadgets will be easier to find!

MAKING THE MOST OF YOUR SEWING SPACE

33

Kitchen Counter Cutting Station

Tip

Consider stock kitchen cabinets for permanent workspace. The height is comfortable for cutting and pressing, and there is ample storage below for baskets and bins.

If you don't have the luxury of a separate sewing space, **the kitchen provides a good alternative for a temporary cutting station.** The area is usually well lit, with lots of outlets and sufficient flat surfaces for cutting and pressing. Sometimes you can even appropriate a bit of drawer or shelf space to store a small mat, cutter, and a ruler or two. Best of all, the work surface is a comfortable height for stand-up work! Just be sure the surface (countertop or island) is wiped clean before you begin.

Rotary-Ruler Organization

Tip

Identify your rulers and other workshop gadgets with adhesive address labels so you don't lose them when you take them to a class. The clear variety work best.

If possible, keep your collection of rotary rulers close to your cutting area. Store rulers—along with cutters, scissors, and spare blades—in a nearby drawer or within easy reach. An inexpensive umbrella stand makes a compact container for long, cumbersome rulers, while a plastic-coated pot lid rack keeps smaller or oddly shaped rulers standing close by. The Ruler Roundup is a great new product to tame unruly rulers.

Rulers can be wall-mounted, as well. Most rotary rulers have a hole in one end. Thread a piece of ribbon or nylon fishing line through the hole, and hang the rulers on a hook or pegboard.

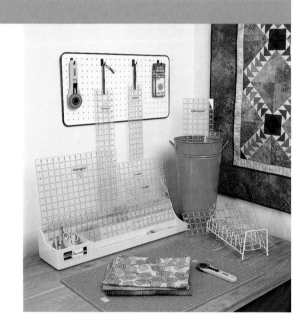

Cutting-Mat Storage

To prevent warping, cutting mats must be stored flat, away from excessive heat and out of direct sunlight. You can store your mats under the bed or sofa, or snugly between cabinets or bookshelves in your sewing space. Just be sure the mat stands straight and doesn't bend, or it may warp.

A clamp-style wooden clothes hanger, such as the type used to hang men's trousers, is ideal for cutting-mat storage. Secure the cutting mat in the hanger and suspend from a hook, in a closet, or even over the back of a door for an inexpensive, space-saving solution.

Organizing & Storing Quilt Patterns

There are loads of efficient—and low-cost—options for organizing and storing quilt patterns. Individual patterns can be sorted by designer, type of project, or motif. Then they can be stored in **accordion files or color-coded file folders. Or, encase them in plastic sleeves, and catalog them in labeled three-ring binders.**

Clasp-style envelopes are another worthy alternative. Brown kraft paper varieties are inexpensive and come in many sizes. Brightly colored plastic types even come portfolio-size, perfect for oversize designs. The latter are also see-through, making identification a snap.

Conquering Quilt Stencils

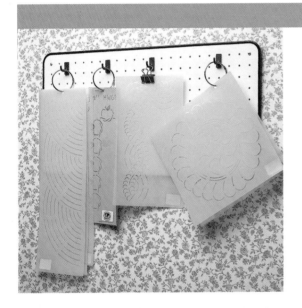

Quilt stencils come in a variety of shapes and sizes. This, coupled with the fact that they are both flexible and slick, can make storage difficult. For an easy, inexpensive solution, visit an office supply store. **Purchase traditional binder clips, bulldog-style clips, or—better still—metal rings to corral cumbersome stencils. Rings come in different sizes, can be purchased individually, and snap open and closed with ease.** Most stencils have prepunched holes; simply separate the stencils by size or motif, and thread them onto the rings. Both rings and clips can then be hung from hooks for easy access.

Organizing Your Quilt Library

Turn an out-of-control library into a valuable resource with these tips:

• **Alphabetize** quilt books by author, or group them by subject.
• **Purchase cardboard magazine holders** at an office supply store or make your own from empty laundry detergent boxes. Separate magazines by title in labeled, dated boxes.
• **Photocopy** the contents pages from books and magazines, and keep them in a three-ring binder.
• **Use labeled self-stick notes** or cut color-coded paper strips to tag items.

MAKING THE MOST OF YOUR SEWING SPACE

Speed-Piecing
Shortcuts

I f quilters were asked to name their most indispensable quilting tool, the rotary cutter would surely be near, if not at the top, of the list. This versatile gadget has revolutionized quiltmaking in the twentieth century much as the sewing machine did 100 years before. Together, the two offer today's busy quiltmaker a myriad of time- and labor-saving choices. The result? More accurate, more complex . . . simply more *wonderful* quilts! In this chapter, author, teacher, and quilter Darra Williamson presents some of her favorite piecing and cutting shortcuts.

Introduction

Some quick-cutting and speed-piecing methods are so familiar that they have become part of our basic quiltmaking vocabulary. *Perfect Piecing,* the first volume in Rodale's Successful Quilting Library, contains detailed instructions for some of these more commonly known techniques, including strip piecing, grid-method triangle squares, and individual, quarter-square, and bias-square triangles. Whether you are a beginner or a more experienced quiltmaker, you'll find it an ideal reference.

This chapter contains some not-so-familiar but equally efficient and accurate methods for piecing those units that appear again and again in both traditional and original quilt designs. Use these methods to put your traditional blocks together quickly, or make the units and have fun mixing and matching them on a design wall to create something completely different. You'll discover uses for leftover strip sets as well as some simple tips for making the "tried-and-true" more up-to-date and versatile.

Speedy Strip Piecing

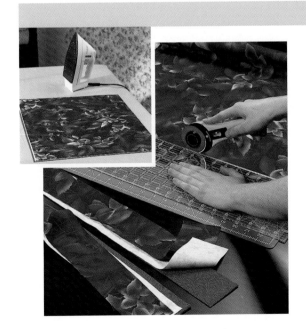

Try these tips to make your basic strip piecing even easier, safer, and more accurate:

• Stack fabrics that will be cut into same-width strips. You can cut three or four layers at a time.
• **Press each stack just before cutting. The layers adhere to each other and shifting is minimized.**
• **Place the fabric on your cutting mat so you can cut by moving the ruler, not the fabric, after each cut.**
• Cut with the bulk of the fabric to your right if you are right-handed, vice versa if you are a lefty.
• Close the blade *every time* you put the cutter down.

Be sure your rotary blade is sharp! A dull blade slows you down, affects precision, and invites injury.

Easy Piecing: Sew First, Cut Later

Tip

As you sew each strip to the strip set, alternate the end at which you begin sewing. This helps control the "curving" or distortion so common in strip piecing.

Some blocks rely on unusual shapes that combine a dark and a light fabric to create the illusion of depth, such as the Mariner's Compass with its long, sharp points. Cutting, then sewing the two required triangles can be tricky. The solution? **Assemble a strip set of the two contrasting fabrics, and press the seam allowance open. Make a see-through template, marking the center seam line in pencil. Position the template with the pencil marking over the seam line of the strip set. Carefully trace and cut the already-sewn unit.**

Quick-Pieced Lone Stars

Tip

Apply a light coating of spray starch to the strip set and press before cutting it into "slices."

By "slicing" strip sets at an angle other than 90 degrees you can construct a familiar block like Lone Star with amazing speed and accuracy. Determine the width of the individual diamond plus its seam allowance, and cut strips of the appropriate fabrics to this width. **Piece strip sets with fabrics in order for *each* diagonal row of the star's large diamond points. Align the 45 degree marking on your ruler with a seam line on each strip set.** Cut "slices" to the finished side measurement of the individual diamond, plus its seam allowance. Arrange and sew the strips to form the large diamond points.

Strip-Pieced Borders and Bindings

Tip

Press each strip as it is added. You'll be amazed at how this simple step improves the overall accuracy of your finished strip sets.

You can strip piece, slice, and re-assemble fabrics for exciting borders and bindings, as well. These borders and bindings are especially effective when the slices are cut on the bias. Follow the instructions for "Quick-Pieced Lone Stars," above, to **cut and assemble the strip sets, arranging the strips in any order you desire. You can cut individual *strips* to any width, but cut *border slices* to the finished width of the border, plus the seam allowance. Cut *binding slices* approximately 2 inches wide.** Join the individual slices into long strips to add instant pizzazz to your quilt!

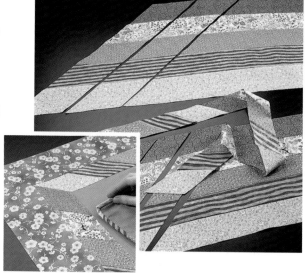

The Square-on-the-Corner Technique

The Square-on-the-Corner piecing technique saves time and effort when a 45 degree (half-square) triangle must be added to a second single shape to form a square or rectangular unit. It is accurate enough for use in miniatures, and is especially efficient when working with true scraps or when the desire for variety eliminates more familiar methods, such as grid or bias-square piecing. **Here are just some of the units that make good candidates for this nifty, quick-cutting, quick-piecing technique.** Many traditional blocks incorporate these units, so the method is as versatile as it is precise.

1

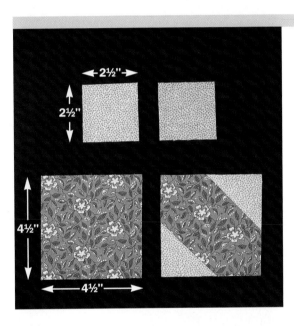

All Square-on-the-Corner pieces are cut as squares and rectangles, so fabrics may be stacked and rotary cut for speed. Cut measurements are based on the finished size of the unit *plus ½ inch*. Determine the size relationship between the half-square triangle and the overall unit. For example, **in a 4-inch finished Indian Hatchet unit, the corner triangle equals half the block's measurement—or 2 inches—along its right angle edge.** Cut two 2½-inch squares (the finished side of the triangle *plus ½ inch*), and one 4½-inch square (the finished measurement of the unit *plus ½ inch*) from a contrasting fabric.

2

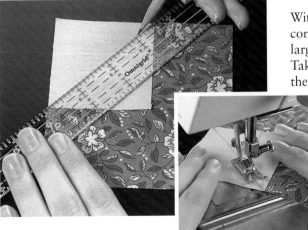

With right sides together, align the corners of the small square and the larger piece (rectangle or square). Take care to place the small square in the position where the half-square triangle should appear in the finished unit. **Use a ruler to draw a pencil line from corner to corner on the small square.** You'll know you've marked correctly if the pencil line "draws in" the triangle as it will appear in the finished unit. **Stitch directly on the pencil line.**

Tip

Two strategically placed pins in the corners opposite the diagonal will hold the pieces in place as you mark and sew them.

Tip

If you lay the lengthwise grain of cut pieces "north and south" when pinning and sewing, you'll avoid problems with directional fabrics.

3

Use scissors or a rotary cutter and ruler to trim the excess from the sewn corner, leaving approximately a ¼-inch seam allowance. **Turn back the newly formed corner, and carefully press the seam allowance toward this new triangle piece.**

4

Repeat Steps 1 through 3 to add any additional corner squares to complete the unit. **Complete one whole corner (marking, stitching, trimming, and pressing) before adding a square to an** *adjacent* **(neighboring) corner of the larger shape.** This eliminates pressing problems with corner triangles that overlap to form seam allowances, as in Flying Geese units. Squares may be marked, stitched, trimmed, and cut at any time when being added to *opposite* (diagonal) corners, such as on the Indian Hatchet block.

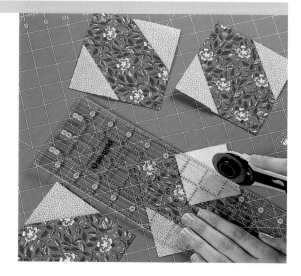

Bonus: Using the Leftovers

If the idea of wasting even the tiniest bit of fabric makes you uneasy, or if you simply want a jump start on your next quilting project, try this tip for utilizing Square-on-the-Corner cutaway pieces. As you mark the sewing line as described in Step 2 on page 39, **draw a second line ½ inch from the first and closer to the corner of the square. Then stitch** *both* **lines.** When you trim away the waste as described in Step 3, you'll be cutting between the two sewn lines. **Fold back and press the cutaway piece toward the darker triangle.** You'll have an already stitched mini half-square triangle!

Mary's Triangles with Squares

Quiltmaker and teacher Sally Schneider came up with this great shortcut for making two 4-inch blocks at a time. She calls them Mary's Triangles with Squares, and they can be used in numerous settings. Cut two $2\frac{1}{2} \times 3\frac{1}{2}$-inch light rectangles, two $2\frac{1}{2}$-inch dark squares, and one $4\frac{1}{2} \times 5\frac{1}{2}$-inch dark rectangle. **Stitch the small squares and rectangles together. Clip the seam allowance to the stitching line in the center of the unit.**

Tip

Make half-square triangle units that measure $2\frac{1}{2}$ inches, and use them in place of the square to make Mary's Triangles with Triangles.

Press the seam away from the squares in opposite directions. Make a triangular template by cutting a $4\frac{1}{2}$-inch square of template material and then cutting it in half diagonally. Place the template on the wrong side of the pieced unit, and draw a diagonal stitching line along the long edge of the template. **Rotate the template to the opposite corner of the unit, and draw a second line.**

Tip

A sheet of fine- or medium-grade sandpaper placed under fabric will keep it from shifting as you mark sewing lines or trace around templates.

Place the remaining dark rectangle right sides together with the pieced rectangle, and stitch on each of the drawn lines. **Use a ruler and rotary cutter to cut between the lines, creating two blocks.**

Easy Mark
Quilting Designs

Marking is one of those tasks that many quilters wish would just take care of itself. It's tedious and time-consuming, and sometimes it's hard to find the right marker. Quilters often choose to follow the path of least resistance—quilting without marking. If you fit that description, you're going to love the great ideas Susan Stein has gathered for no-mark quilting. Plus, we've added some ingenious ways to mark with as little effort as possible.

On Your Mark, Get Set, Quilt

Stitchable Stencils

Stitchable stencils allow you to machine quilt motifs without marking. (See "Quilter's Marketplace" on page 124 for more information.) The designs are laser cut into thin paper, much like a traditional plastic stencil. Only small bridges of paper hold the stencil together, so after you follow the easy-to-see lines with your stitching, the bridges release effortlessly. The designs range from 4 to 6½ inches. Some of the patterns can be cut in half and used for borders. Simply pin the paper at the corners before stitching.

Use a quilt basting spray to stick tissue paper patterns and stencils to your quilt while you are stitching. Spray the paper in a well-ventilated room.

Con-Tact Paper Stencils

Make a stencil out of Con-Tact paper for no-mark quilting. This works best if the motif is a solid space with an outline, rather than a complex design. **Cut out a shape and stick it onto the quilt where you want to stitch.** Clear Con-Tact will allow you to see through it for placement, but a pattern or color will be easier to follow when stitching. **Quilt around the motif, ¹⁄₁₆ inch away from the edge to avoid getting adhesive on your needle.** After you are finished, carefully peel the stencil off and reposition it. When the stencil loses its stickiness, cut another one.

Test the Con-Tact paper first to determine whether the stencil will pull any batting through the fabric of your quilt top.

Marking a Grid

To mark grids in background areas, try the June Tailor Grid Marker. This 11½ × 19½-inch plastic sheet is slotted in half-inch increments so you can run your favorite marking device through the grooves at whatever spacing you desire for your grid. There are also 30, 45, and 60 degree markings for diamond grids. Use this tool for small areas that need dense background quilting in order to highlight appliqué or fancy quilting patterns.

Check your local quilt shop regularly to see what new gadgets are available to make marking your quilt easier.

EASY MARK QUILTING DESIGNS

43

Quilt Stencil Transfer Pad

Years ago, quilters used cornstarch, powder, cocoa, or cinnamon as "pouncing powder" with paper stencils to transfer complex designs to their quilts for hand quilting. This old idea has been updated with **a new tool, the quilt stencil transfer pad. It is filled with loose chalk through a convenient reservoir opening in the top and wiped over a sturdy plastic quilting stencil for bold lines.** The chalk comes off the fabric easily after quilting, and refills are available in blue or white.

Free-Motion Quilting by Eye

Tip

If you are doing free-motion stippling, warm up first on a "doodle cloth." Free-motion quilting can be hard to rip out.

On a quilt where the emphasis is on piecing or appliqué, **outline the motifs or shapes and quilt the background freehand by machine.** Use a stipple design, an allover leaf pattern, stars connected with curvy lines, a triangular stipple pattern, loops, or roughly parallel, irregularly spaced parallel lines. Use a walking foot for parallel lines and a darning foot for circular patterns. Another option is to quilt around the patterns in the fabrics, highlighting the motifs. Relax and play with new patterns. The idea is to have fun and finish the quilt, not to make every stitch perfect and every quilt worthy of a large cash award!

Wash-Away Plastic

Try wash-away plastic for marking the stitching lines prior to machine quilting. Wash-away plastic is like a sandwich bag in weight and stays in sheet form as long as it is dry. Water will dissolve it, removing your stencil at the same time you launder your quilt. **Draw the quilting design on the plastic with a white opaque pen or black permanent marker.** The marker will adhere to the plastic and will not harm the quilt. Pin the plastic to the quilt and stitch over the lines. Remove large pieces of plastic by hand before laundering.

Foundation-Piecing Paper as Stencils

There are hundreds of foundation-piecing designs in print and on computer programs. Take these same designs and use the papers for machine quilting. **Pin the paper design where you wish, quilt on the piecing lines, and rip the paper off.** If a design is too small for your project, enlarge the motif on a copy machine and then trace it onto tissue paper.

Stitching from the Back

Choose a backing fabric that has large, distinct motifs printed on it. Wind the bobbin of the machine with thread that you want to show on the top of the quilt, and turn the quilt over to machine quilt it. **Outline the motif on the backing fabric to create the pattern on the front.** This technique allows you to use thicker threads that would not go through the top of the machine and the needle. You may need to loosen the screw on the bobbin case to adjust the tension. If you like this technique, you may want to get an extra bobbin case for specialty threads.

Tip

Look for large floral or leafy designs or geometric prints that allow you to quilt on the diagonal or around repeated curved patterns.

Full-Size Quilting Pattern

Hang the finished quilt top on a design wall and cover it with a thin plastic drop cloth. **With a washable marker, draw a full-size quilting design to enhance the pattern of the quilt top.** If you want to change a line, wipe it off with a damp paper towel. You may use the pattern simply as a reference for free-hand quilting, or lay a piece of Saral transfer paper under it and trace the lines onto the fabric. If you prefer, place tracing paper over the plastic. Draw quilting lines with a permanent marker, pin the tracing paper to the quilt, stitch through the paper, and tear it off afterward.

Tip

Saral transfer paper can be found in quilt shops and art supply stores.

EASY MARK QUILTING DESIGNS

Combination Quilting

For an exciting (and quick!) sampler quilt, use large-print fabrics in place of some of the pieced blocks. **Then ditch-quilt the sampler blocks and outline the print motifs on the other blocks. This works well for print borders, too.** Borders sometimes get neglected in an effort to complete a quilt. Double Wedding Rings look great with ditch quilting in the seams of the rings and free-motion quilting around the motifs in the open areas. Probably the most popular use of motif quilting is in a baby quilt, often made with a printed panel of animals, clowns, or other juvenile designs.

Tracing Geometric Shapes

Tip

Look in a child's coloring book for simple shapes that will work well as quilting designs.

Challenge yourself to come up with a quilting design using only your piecing and appliqué templates and measuring tools. A heart template overlapped along a border works well, and is especially easy to mark if you vary the spacing of the hearts. A triangle or diamond template can be used to draw scattered, overlapping, or chained patterns, either in blocks or in a border. Give a shape to a member of the family and see what they come up with for ideas. Some patterns may need a guideline to keep them straight, while others can be random, depending on the degree of formality you want.

Square Rotary Rulers

Use square rotary rulers to create border designs or allover designs of overlapping and interlocking squares. Use a variety of sizes or stick to one size, depending on the size of your quilt or the blocks. Do a rough sketch on plain paper to determine spacing if you want a uniform look. For a more contemporary, random, or irregular look, just start marking!

The Quilter's
Problem Solver

Solving the Quilting Dilemma

How do you decide what quilting design to use for a specific project? Ask yourself these questions:

1. Does the pattern require the secondary design of a distinct quilting treatment, or is ditch quilting all it needs?
2. Does the pattern need the softening effect of curved quilting designs, rather than straight-line patterns?
3. Do I want this quilt to look traditional, with the use of cables, feathers, and other fancy patterns?
4. What kinds of patterns am I attracted to in other people's quilts?
5. Would the quilt design be enhanced by the addition of overall curved lines, as in an underwater scene or windy landscape?
6. Will the quilting support what I'm trying to say in the quilt?
7. Do I want to highlight certain areas and heavily quilt down the background with stippling or echo quilting?
8. Do I want to do continuous-line machine stitching or hand-stitched designs using small, traditional stitches?
9. Will the stitching show up on the fabrics I've used, or will fancy quilting get lost?
10. Does the batting I've chosen require lots of quilting for durability, or can the quilting be spaced farther apart?
11. How is the quilt going to be used, and will it be washed often?
12. Does the end use of the quilt justify many hours of quilting, or is minimal time expenditure prudent? Is it better to finish the project quickly?
13. What do I enjoy doing—piecing, appliqué, embroidery, and so on—or is the quilting the best part of the project?
14. How will I feel when I look at this quilt in the future—did I do it justice?
15. Does the design I'm considering fill all the space, or does it leave open areas that will look unfinished?
16. Does the quilting design seem to be in the same scale with the piecing or appliqué patterns?
17. Is the quilting design too fussy or feminine for the piecing?
18. Does the quilting design detract from the impact of the piecing/appliqué? Does it seem like an afterthought?
19. Does the quilting treatment cover the whole quilt with a consistent density of stitching so that the quilt doesn't pucker or ripple?
20. Would decorative threads, sashiko, or "big stitches" complement the quilt?

EASY MARK QUILTING DESIGNS

47

Pressing
Pointers

As in every aspect of quiltmaking, there are many opinions on the subject of pressing. Some quilters shun steam entirely, while others wouldn't press without it. Some quilters press seams to one side, some press them open. At any rate, pressing is important, but as quilt teacher Susan Stein emphasizes, it should be done with a light hand, "as if you were pressing butterfly wings." Read on for some tips about the ups, downs, and "slideways" of the practice of pressing.

Pressing Tips

Pressing Pieced Units

When pressing seams, **press units with straight-of-grain edges only. Any patches with unsewn bias edges should not be pressed until they are further contained.** That may mean that some seams are not pressed until they are sewn into a squared-off subsection of the block.

Tip

When piecing a flower or star, press the seam allowances toward the shape that you want to highlight. This also makes background quilting easier.

Pressing Triangle Squares

For quilt designer and teacher Sharon Hultgren, perfect piecing is a "pressing" matter. She suggests that when pressing triangle squares you **keep the darker fabric on top. When the triangle square is flopped open the seam allowance will be pressed toward the darker fabric.** If you do this so that the seam allowance is toward the left, the iron works right into the seam and doesn't create a pleat. Position the next triangle square with your left hand while the right hand is pressing the previous one.

Tip

Spray finished quilt blocks with a light coating of starch before pressing. The starch will help to stabilize the block and minimize stretching.

Pressing Appliqué

Appliqué looks best when it is not smashed down with the iron. Use a light touch and avoid pressing so hard that seam allowances on the back make an imprint on the top. Use a press cloth or a piece of cooking parchment to prevent making shiny spots on thicker areas, or **place the block on a terry towel and iron from the back.** If an area looks overpressed, spray it with cool water and let it dry.

PRESSING POINTERS

The Open & Closed Controversy

Tip

If you discover that you've pressed a seam the wrong way, first press it back to its prepressed state. Then press in the opposite direction.

There are two schools of thought on pressing seams. One says that seams pressed open will be flatter and easier to match. Open seams can be ditch quilted exactly down the line of stitching. The other school says that **seams pressed to one side will be easier to match because they lock together when they oppose each other.** This works especially well for designs like Flying Geese, Trip Around the World, or Irish Chain, and it allows you to skip pinning every intersection. Ditch quilting will be hidden by the ridge on the opposite side of the seam line.

Pressing Curved Seams

Press curved seams toward the shape you want to highlight or in the direction that will cause the least puckering. In the case of a Double Wedding Ring or other pieced pattern, choose either the rings or the background fabric, and press all of the seams in that direction. It is very distracting to see seams on a regular pattern going in different directions. Sharp curves will press most easily from the front, using the tip of the iron snug up against the ridge of the seam line.

Pressing a Large Top

Use the square end of the ironing board and press half of the quilt top at a time. Another option is to cover your cutting table or countertop with thick towels and iron on top of that. Be very careful that the surface of the table or countertop does not get hot since extreme heat can unglue the Formica surface on countertops. Press the quilt top on the back first to make sure all seam allowances are lying flat and all dark threads are removed. Then press from the right side to make sure there are no pleats along the seams.

Pressing a Finished Quilt

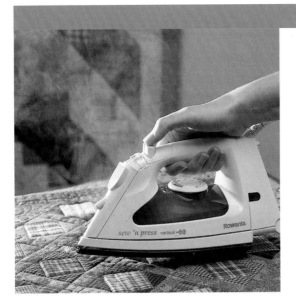

If you use cotton or a cotton/polyester blend batting, there is no harm in lightly pressing a finished quilt. To block a quilt that doesn't quite lie flat, or to neaten a quilt that has just been washed, **fill the iron with water and lightly press the surface of the quilt with lots of steam. Lay the quilt out flat to completely dry before handling it. Do not press a quilt with polyester batting.** The batting will melt easily. If the quilt has a polyester batt or if you're uncertain whether it's cotton or polyester, place the quilt on the floor, mist it with cold water, and let it dry flat.

Squaring Up a Block with Freezer Paper

If you have blocks that are slightly irregular in shape, here's a way to press them so they will be square. Cut a square of freezer paper the size the unfinished block is supposed to be. Press it onto the ironing board cover. **Pin one of the sewn blocks to the ironing board cover, exactly matching its edges with the corners and edges of the freezer paper. Steam the block, letting it fully dry before unpinning it.**

Using a Gridded Ironing Board Cover

If you often have blocks that are not square, it might be wise to **invest in a gridded ironing board cover. It has printed lines that allow you to straighten your blocks by pinning them to the cover and steaming them into shape.** Let them dry before removing them. The cover will also help you keep strip sets from developing curves when pressing the seam allowances.

Ironing on the Road

Tip

Be careful if you are using a towel for an ironing surface—the steam goes right through the towel and may damage the surface underneath.

To iron in a class or while vacationing, plan ahead for your pressing needs. Consider purchasing a small board with a cutting mat on one side to save space in your suitcase and on the table. There are also miniature ironing boards with a point on one end and short legs that raise the board above table level. An ironing blanket folds up and can be used on any surface. Be aware that some seminars ban the use of travel irons in class, so you may want to choose a full-size, lightweight iron. Many hotels will provide ironing boards, presumably to prevent burn marks on the carpeting!

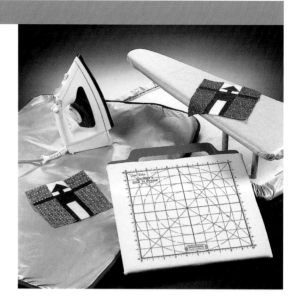

Using a Big Board

If you want a really large ironing surface, you might want to purchase a Big Board. These 22 × 60-inch boards fit on top of a standard ironing board. They greatly increase pressing capabilities (you will be able to iron 45-inch wide yardage in one pass) but do not require any clamps, so they can be easily removed when you want to use the point on the regular ironing board. Check your local quilt shop, mail order catalogs, or the Internet for these boards. (See page 88 in "Time-Shavers" for information on making your own.)

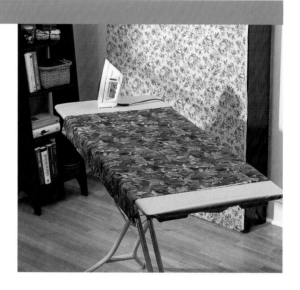

Chair Level Ironing

Place your ironing board next to your chair and lower it to table height so that you can press seams without getting up. Or set up your portable ironing surface on the sewing table, being careful to place the iron where you will not brush against it. A TV tray will also work. Keep in mind, however, that getting up to press is a form of exercise that many of us could benefit from!

The Quilter's
Problem Solver

Choosing the Right Iron

There are lots of opinions about irons, but the trend now seems to be away from expensive European models and back to lower-priced irons. Some people like old irons and search for them at garage and yard sales. They are hunting for those that have really smooth surfaces without steam holes. These are great for fusing since steam holes can mar the bonding of fusible adhesives. If they want steam, they use a spray bottle to dampen the fabric.

Other quilters like irons that produce lots of steam. Some irons have a spray feature built into the front of the iron for spot dampening when steam alone is inadequate. One contingent of quilters favors a heavy iron that does the hard work for them, while many prefer a lightweight iron to prevent wrist fatigue.

An iron should have adequate steam holes, a gauge to tell when the water is running low, and a tip sharp enough to go into corners and between appliqué motifs. An automatic shut-off feature may not be desirable for quilters. It can be very annoying if you go to press seams and find that your iron has shut off.

If you do a lot of fusible appliqué or heat setting of paints and foils, look for an iron with a non-stick surface.

If you have room for a large ironing setup in your studio, you may want to build a permanent pressing station. See page 33 in "Making the Most of Your Sewing Space." Instead of filing cabinets, Susan Stein suggests wire racks with drawers that are a few inches shorter than the height you would like the ironing board to be. Set up two of these rack units under the wooden door, and fill the drawers with projects and notions.

For serious pressing centers, you may want to buy a professional iron with the water reservoir that hangs overhead. This allows you to get major steam action without having to fill the iron. Other things to consider are pressing units that resemble the ones at dry cleaners and old fashioned mangles.

PRESSING POINTERS

Care & Feeding
of Your Quilts

Whether you've created your own quilt, inherited it (lucky you!), or purchased a well-loved antique from a dealer, you'll need to give it all the tender, loving care it deserves so that it will be around for generations to come. Here are some helpful ways to ensure that it will be handed down through your family in the best possible condition. Our panel of writers includes well-known quilters Nancy O'Bryant Puentes, Janet Wickell, and Jane Hall.

Quilt Care 101

Nancy O'Bryant Puentes, author and authority on quilt care and conservation, suggests that you consider your quilts to be members of your family. That will steer you in the right direction when it comes to caring for them. Don't keep them where it's too hot, too cold, too humid, or where pests can get to them. Keep them clean, but don't wash them unless you really need to. Great care should be taken in deciding whether to wash an antique quilt, but most contemporary quilts can be washed carefully. Hand washing is preferable and highly recommended. If you must use a washing machine, use gentle agitation and spin to remove excess water. Dry flat; do not dry in a dryer. Consistent watchfulness and preventive maintenance will guarantee that your quilts will last a long time and will minimize the need for restoration. Refer to "Before You Hang Your Quilt Checklist" on page 67 for a list of things to consider when you plan to display a quilt. When storing quilts, refold two to three times a year, and check for pests and other damage. Air quilts and lay them flat at least once a year.

Check before You Wash

If your quilt dates from the last quarter of the nineteenth century, has been washed before, *and* is in very good condition, it is probably safe to hand wash it in your tub in cool water. If it appears that the quilt has never been washed, you must first test every fabric for colorfastness. Chemical dyes emerged during this era, and they were often unstable. **Rub a damp cotton swab across each fabric. If dye transfers to the tip of the swab, you know the fabric will bleed when wet.**

Synthrapol for Washing Quilts

When washing an antique quilt or a new quilt for the first time, add Synthrapol to the water. **This liquid solution suspends dye particles in the water, keeping them from settling on and staining other fabrics.** Remove as much moisture from the quilt as possible, then air-dry, using a fan to speed up the process. There's less chance of dye transfer when fabrics dry quickly. Dyes that have already transferred are not always "set." When washed again, they often disappear—and Synthrapol in the wash helps prevent a reoccurrence of the problem.

Tip

If your quilt is creased, Gloria Hansen suggests washing it and smoothing the crease as much as possible while the quilt is damp.

Neutralize Chlorine

Does your washer smell like a swimming pool when you fill it with water? If it does, your water has a high chlorine content, which could lead to dye loss in any quilts you launder. High levels of chlorine in tap water can cause bleeding in some fabrics. **A cup of vinegar in the wash water will help neutralize chlorine and minimize dye loss.**

Prevent Bleeding Thread & Color Transfer

Tip

When laundering quilts, use fans if necessary to speed up the drying process.

Some threads bleed dye when they become damp. To check for this before stitching, cut a short length of thread and **submerge it in soapy water. Rinse. Place the damp thread on a white paper towel, and press it between two layers to see if dye transfer occurs.**

Color transference can take place where quilting stitches pinch together the layers of a quilt. The compression may lead to dye transfer along the stitches, especially if a laundered quilt remains damp for some time. Remove as much moisture from laundered quilts as possible, then air-dry.

Vacuuming Quilts

Vacuuming is the least stressful way to clean a quilt, and it removes a great deal of dust and dirt. Spread the quilt on a bed or table. Prepare a square of fiberglass or nylon screening (about 2 × 2 feet) by covering the rough edges with cotton twill tape or duct tape. **Place the screen over the quilt; hold it securely so the quilt isn't sucked into the vacuum. Use a vacuum with an upholstery attachment. Cover the opening of the attachment with several layers of cheesecloth, nylon tulle, or old pantyhose.** Vacuum both sides thoroughly using the lowest suction setting.

Tip

If your quilt is hanging on the wall, you can vacuum it there.

Fade Your Fabrics

If you need to repair or replace fabrics in an antique quilt, **you can quickly "age" a new fabric to fit in by placing it in a sunny window for several days.** The sun will fade the fabric and give it an old look quickly. This will also demonstrate the importance of keeping quilts and fabrics out of the sun if you *don't* want them to fade.

Handy Storage Box Kits

For safe, secure storage of your antique or heirloom quilts, you may want to consider purchasing acid-free boxes and tissue paper or quilt storage kits. For long-term acid-free products, ask for lignin-free as well as acid-free tissue paper and boxes. Ideally, quilts should be inspected and refolded three times a year. Label the box and record on it the dates when the quilt was last checked and refolded. **The Forever Box, a quilt storage kit available from Craftgard (see "Quilter's Marketplace" on page 124), consists of an acid-free storage box and neutral tissue paper for cushioning folds.**

Tip

Nancy Kirk recommends nonbuffered tissue paper for quilting cottons and buffered tissue paper for wool and silk.

CARE & FEEDING OF YOUR QUILTS

Filter the Light

Fluorescent lights mimic the short-wave ultraviolet rays that cause the most damage to fabric and other materials. Placing ultraviolet filters over the lights won't stop the deterioration, but will slow it down considerably. **Purchase the plastic sleeves at an electrical supply house, and slip them over the bulbs.** If you are building a new home or replacing windows, you can purchase windows that are designed to reduce ultraviolet radiation, as well.

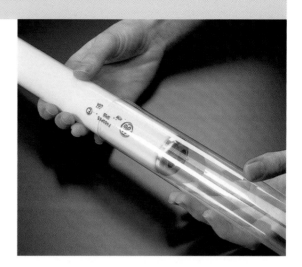

Bolsters for Folding

If you run out of special tissue paper to pad your quilts when you store them, here's an alternative. **Make several bolsters quickly from leftover lengths of cotton muslin and quilt batting scraps. Roll the muslin around the batting, and tie the ends of the bolsters with cotton twill tape.** Make enough to pad your quilt.

Protect Your Quilts

To protect your quilts and quilt projects from stains, moisture, and fading, try using one of two fairly new products, Craftgard or Quiltgard. Craftgard protects fabrics by repelling dirt and liquid spills. It also strengthens fibers for longer wear. Quiltgard does the same thing, but also protects quilts and textiles from ultraviolet light to retard fading. Both products are acid free, will not change the look or feel of fabric, **and will cause water and other liquids to bead up and not soak in. Spray the quilt, and allow it to dry and cure over a period of 48 to 72 hours.**

Stain, Stain, Go Away

For any stain, act quickly (while it is fresh if possible). Try the simplest method listed here first—cool water and mild rubbing. Do not use hot water on an unknown stain. Rinse well and launder after any treatment.

Stain	Treatment Options
Baby urine, feces, vomit, liquid vitamins	1. Rinse immediately with cool water. 2. Treat with liquid detergent and/or nonchlorine bleach. Rinse thoroughly and wash with enzyme-containing detergent. 3. Try a protein stain remover, found at maternity or fabric stores.
Ballpoint pen or marker	1. Wet the fabric with cool water. Apply glycerine (available from a drugstore) and let stand 20 minutes. Rub in a small amount of detergent and rinse thoroughly. 2. Spray a small amount of hairspray on the mark. Rub gently, rinse well, and wash with detergent. 3. Apply alcohol immediately to ballpoint ink. Rinse well.
Cat/dog urine, vomit	1. Rinse immediately with cool water 2. Since urine is an acid, apply an alkali (solution of ammonia or sprinkle of baking soda). A solution of one-half cup of salt in a quart of water may be effective. Rinse well and launder with detergent. 3. Treat with liquid detergent and/or nonchlorine bleach (Vivid, Biz). Rinse thoroughly and launder with detergent
Coffee or tea	1. Pour boiling water over the fabric from a 12-inch height, rub gently, and repeat if necessary. 2. Wash with enzyme-containing detergent, using nonchlorine bleach if necessary 3. Try Spray 'n Wash laundry booster. 4. Treat with club soda, rinse, and launder with detergent
Fruit or berry juice	1. Pour boiling water over the fabric from a height of 2 to 3 feet. Rub gently, repeat if necessary. 2. Treat with nonchlorine bleach and then launder with detergent.
Red wine	1. Wet the fabric with cool water, and rub gently. 2. Treat with nonchlorine bleach or oxygen bleach, and then launder with detergent. 3. Blot stain, sprinkle with white wine, blot again. Rinse well. 4. Pour boiling water over the fabric from a 12-inch height.
Grease or oil spots	1. Use a laundry product especially for grease removal 2. Use a shampoo for oily hair. 3. Sprinkle grease spot with cornstarch, leave overnight. Shake, rinse, and launder.
Mildew	1. Brush off loose mildew, shake quilt, and launder with detergent. 2. Treat stubborn stains with nonchlorine bleach 3. Apply lemon juice and salt, and let sit in sunlight. This may lighten spots.
Scorch marks	1. Rinse the area with cool water immediately, rubbing lightly. 2. If stains persist, treat with nonchlorine bleach and launder with an enzyme-containing detergent.

Note: There are a myriad of commercial products in grocery and drug stores. When using any of these, test them first on an inconspicuous spot. *Always* take care not to be too zealous—work slowly, sparingly, and carefully. Old or severe stains sometimes cannot be removed without taking some of the threads of the fabric with them.

CARE & FEEDING OF YOUR QUILTS

Displaying &
Decorating

It's exciting when you near the end of a quilting project. When that last stitch is taken, you can truly see the results of your work. Now it's time to share it with friends and family. In this chapter, Janet Wickell—quilter, miniaturist, teacher, and author—suggests creative ways to hang and display quilts in your home. Here you'll find many options for making the most of your collection when decorating. Be sure to read "Before You Hang Your Quilt Checklist" on page 67, and don't hesitate to show off your quilts with style!

Hanging Tips

More than One Sleeve

If your quilt is multi-directional, meaning that it can be hung in different directions, **sew sleeves to two or more sides.** Rotate the quilt occasionally to reduce constant stress to any one area of fabrics, seams, and batting.

Velcro Hangers

It is sometimes more difficult to hang a quilt with irregular edges. **If your quilt is heavy, sew a traditional sleeve to the back, then use a flat dowel in the sleeve to make the quilt hang close to the wall. Add small bits of Velcro to areas that tend to sag forward, placing the corresponding "sticky" piece on the wall to hold the edges in place.** For small, lightweight quilts, you can likely skip the sleeve and use only the Velcro for support. It's best to sew a few layers of buffer fabric between the Velcro and the quilt, to help protect it from chemicals that may leach from the Velcro.

Tip

Avoid hanging the quilt in humid locations where moisture can linger between the Velcro and the quilt.

Temporary Rods

Try tension rods when you need to hang a quilt in an area temporarily, or when it's not practical to drill holes, such as to cover the front of a fireplace during summer months. You can use tension rods between moldings on windows and doors, or between the brackets of a wall shelf.

Wooden Rods & Dowels

Large wooden rods, such as those used in closets, make sturdy hangers for large, heavy quilts. They typically have eye hooks at each end, which makes it easy to suspend the quilt from the ceiling or hang it on nails in the wall. **Always paint wooden rods with a few coats of polyurethane, to keep acids in the wood from leaching into your fabrics. Covering wooden rods with aluminum foil is another way to keep acids from touching your fabrics.**

Flat Hangers

Some quilts hang smoother when a flat device is used in the sleeve. **Flat, wooden moldings are available in a variety of widths, and it's easy to trim their length to fit your quilt sleeve.** For small quilts with thin strips, rest molding ends on nails or brackets in the wall. For larger quilts, drill holes in molding ends and hang with nails or screws. Be sure to coat wooden moldings with polyurethane to protect your quilt from acids that could leach from the wood.

Plexiglas Hangers

Cut a strip of Plexiglas to insert through your quilt sleeve. Plexiglas is a sturdy, inert substance that will not leach harmful chemicals onto your fabrics. Drill a hole in each end of the strip, then use nails or screws to hang the quilt on a wall.

You may be able to purchase scraps of already-cut Plexiglas that will work fine for hanging quilts.

Hanging Quilts on Metal

Cut a flexible strip magnet slightly shorter than the width of your quilt. Encase it in a fabric sleeve slightly wider than the width of the magnet. Align the top of the sleeve with the top edge of the quilt, and blind stitch around all edges. Use a loosely woven fabric for the magnet to be most effective. Larger, heavier quilts might need extra magnets and sleeves to support their weight.

Tip

Purchase flexible magnet strips at home supply and hardware stores.

Decorative Wire Hangers

A quick, easy, and cute way to display small quilts is to choose from a wide variety of wire hangers that are available in quilt shops and mail order catalogs. Most have pictorial scenes positioned above the quilt hanger. Hanging devices may be a wire rod that slips through the quilt, or a series of clips. These are especially nice for seasonal wallhangings. They make it easy to rotate quilts as often as you like.

Hanging Yo-Yo Quilts

Sewing a sleeve to a yo-yo quilt that does not have the traditional three layers is a challenge. **One option is to sew a piece of Velcro across the top row of yo-yos, hiding it behind junctions where they are joined. To protect the quilt, insert a narrow strip of cotton fabric between the Velcro and the backing.** Attach the corresponding piece of Velcro to the wall, and press in place. Add additional rows of Velcro as needed to support the quilt. Do not hang it in a room with high humidity. You want to be sure no moisture is trapped between the Velcro and the quilt.

Tip

To support a yo-yo quilt for hanging, consider adding a backing fabric and a sleeve. The fabric will peek through between the yo-yos.

DISPLAYING & DECORATING

63

Wooden Clamp Hangers

Several companies sell decorative hangers that clamp the top edge of a quilt between two pieces of wood. To protect the quilt from materials that may leach from the wood, insert aluminum foil or strips of white fabric between the quilt and both sides of the hanger. Wash the buffering fabric periodically to remove residue.

Creative Display Ideas

Furniture

Draping your quilts over the backs of chairs and sofas is a great way to display them. **Fold a quilt and hang it over the end of a cabinet or a door.** Anything at eye level will become a focal point in the room. Move the quilts around periodically, especially if they are folded, so creases do not become set in any one position.

Decorative Ladders & Fixtures

Antique shops are a good resource for unusual display fixtures. That old washboard sitting in the corner would be more interesting with a quilt draped over it. You might find a print drying rack with wooden dowels just right for hanging a quilt, or you might stumble onto an old tobacco rack. Keep display ideas tucked in mind; you never know when the perfect fixture will pop up.

Containers

Baskets, stone crocks, metal bins, decorative tins—you can make a creative display from just about any container. Roll quilts and insert them side-by-side on end, or drape them to flow out of the container. Place a quilt under a basket of dried flowers, or arrange a collection of old-fashioned tins on top. The more quilts you make, the more ways you'll find to display them.

Children's Furniture

Use children's outgrown furniture as backdrops for quilts. Small chairs, tables, desks, wagons, and other items make great quilt display areas. If you have a crib in a guest room, use that for quilt storage and display when it's not in use.

If you have a fragile or antique yo-yo quilt, display it flat, either on a bed or a piece of furniture.

Doll Furniture

Use a vintage doll cradle, bed, or table and chairs to show off a stack of small quilts. **Lay a quilt out flat with a child's tea set on it for a display with collectible stuffed animals.**

DISPLAYING & DECORATING

Framing Quilt Blocks & Small Quilts

Tip

Framing without glass will allow the fabric to breathe, but will not protect it from dust and dirt. Vacuum occasionally as described on page 57.

Framing is another option for small quilts and blocks. It's best to have a professional framer do the job using conservation glass and a museum-quality mat, one that is acid-free and made of cotton rather than wood fibers. The frame should provide enough depth so that there is some air space between the glass and the fabric. Place information about the quilt in an envelope and seal it behind the board used to back the quilt, before the paper is applied. This will help make sure that the history of the quilt and its maker will be known years from now.

The Quilt Is the Theme

Have fun and be creative with your quilts. Use the pattern to accessorize and create a still-life tableau. Use a miniature quilt with miniature holiday decorations. Stack up vintage building blocks with a four-patch or nine-patch quilt. Build a house of Lincoln logs to go with a Log Cabin quilt. Arrange an assortment of baskets with a basket block quilt. Arrange collectible bears on a simple quilt for a teddy bears' picnic.

Take Your Cue from Color

Play off the color scheme of your quilt. **Hang or display it, and group lots of fun items that match the colors of the fabrics.** Include a bouquet of fresh or dried flowers in the same color palette.

The Quilter's
Problem Solver

Smooth Hanging

Problem	Solution
Quilt doesn't hang smoothly.	Make sure the sleeve is sewn securely to the backing along its top and bottom edges, and along the side edges that touch the backing.
Hanging sleeve is visible above the quilt's top edge.	Use flat wooden lath in the sleeve, rather than a round rod that could cause the sleeve fabric to peek over the quilt's top edge. Make sure you have a horizontal pleat in the hanging sleeve before sewing the bottom of the tube to the backing. This will allow for the depth of the rod. Or, the pleat may need to be wider to allow more depth for a large rod.
The quilt was attached to a wall with straight pins, and now it is distorted along the edges.	Avoid pinning a quilt to a wall, even during its construction. The unsupported areas between pins are pulled down by the weight of the quilt, resulting in distortion that may be permanent. To try solving the problem, lay the quilt flat, mist it with cool water, and gently reshape it to be square. Let it dry thoroughly before moving it.

Before You Hang Your Quilt Checklist

Is the room hot or humid?
❑ Long periods of excessive heat will weaken fabrics. Avoid hanging your quilts near direct heat sources.
❑ Mildew can easily grow on quilts hung in rooms that tend to be damp, such as bathrooms and some areas of kitchens.

Will the quilt be hung in direct sunlight?
❑ Choose another location if possible. It doesn't take long for sunlight to fade fabrics.
❑ Hang a window shade to help block the light.
❑ Cover windows or skylights with a thin, filmlike filter. The filter adheres to the glass and helps block ultraviolet light. Filters are available at most home improvement stores.

What about fluorescent and incandescent lights?
❑ Place filters over fluorescent lights, if possible. They won't eliminate fading, but they will slow it down considerably.
❑ Try to hang quilts at least 10 feet from incandescent lights.
❑ Point recessed or track lights away from your quilts.

Quilting
à la Carte

O ne of the joys of quiltmaking is the absence of many rigid prescriptions. Each quilter is free to determine the design, technique, and method of construction for a particular quilt. You can pick your techniques "à la carte," as you do food from a menu in a restaurant. In that spirit, Jane Hall, quilter, author, and quilt-show judge, avoids judgmental, subjective dos and don'ts in this chapter. Instead, she offers some very relevant, real-life suggestions that you can add to your quiltmaking repertoire.

Safe Rotary Cutting

Holding a Rotary Cutter

If you hold the rotary cutter properly, cutting will be smooth, quick, and easy. **Place the handle firmly in the palm of your dominant hand, with your index finger on the ridged area leading up to the blade.**

Cut Away

Never cut *toward* yourself when using the rotary cutter. By cutting away, you can control the direction of the blade more easily and apply more pressure on the rotary cutter, since a pushing motion is stronger than a pulling one. One small slip can result in a major injury. **Learn to cut *away* from your body, and always cut standing up rather than sitting down.** You have more leverage to operate the cutter and are in a better position to steady the ruler with your other hand. In addition, your cut will be more accurate since you will be able to see the edge of the fabric and the ruler marks both before and after the cut.

Tip

Practice making long, clean cuts, rather than short, choppy ones. A sawing motion with the cutter will produce a roughly cut edge.

The Other Hand

Stabilize the position of the ruler with your weight on your noncutting hand. **It is wise to spread your fingers if the ruler is wide enough, letting one finger rest off the ruler and on the fabric to further brace the ruler.** *Don't* place your fingers or thumb close to the "cutting" edge of the ruler. You risk nicking a digit in the process of rotary cutting. When you have cut as far as you comfortably can, "walk" your stabilizing hand up the ruler to the next position.

QUILTING À LA CARTE

Skipped Threads

If your rotary cutter leaves a thread uncut at regular intervals, the blade is damaged, most likely from running over a pin. Rotary blade sharpeners are sold in quilt and fabric shops, to smooth out nicks and scratches. However, if you are unable to fix the blade, replace it. The aggravation caused by the uncut threads is not worth putting up with. You can also check the classified ads in quilt magazines for rotary cutter blade repair and sharpening services. Check "Quilter's Marketplace" on page 124 for a source of blade sharpeners.

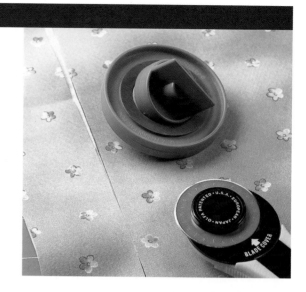

A Proper Fold

Tip

The lines on your cutting mat can be helpful when lining up your fabric prior to cutting.

To make accurate rotary cuts on folded fabric, you must have a 90 degree angle at the horizontal and vertical edges. **Some quilters tear their fabric to find the true woven horizontal line and then fold the fabric vertically, lining up the torn edges.** The selvages may or may not line up, depending on the weave of the particular fabric, but the angle where the folded edge meets the torn edge should be 90 degrees. **Other quilters prefer to line up the selvages, press the fold, and make a straightening cut at a 90 degree angle to the fold before rotating the fabric for cutting strips.**

Square & Square Again

Don't assume that your fabric, once squared, will remain so. **It is necessary to check the angle of the cut edge after every few cuts.** Fabric, as well as the ruler, can slip during the cutting process. **If the angle becomes distorted, the strips will not be straight and you will produce Vs.** Although fabric folded lengthwise twice is easier to handle, it can produce double Vs easily, too. Many quilters prefer to use only one fold, to maintain the most control.

Use the Ruler, Not the Grid

If you usually line up your fabric on a gridded cutting mat and try to cut an accurate strip, *stop*. **Use the ruler rather than the grid on the mat as your cutting guide.** The lines on the mat are useful for lining up the folded edge of fabric, but not nearly as accurate as the lines printed on the ruler. If you are right-handed, place the bulk of the fabric you will be cutting from to the back or toward the right. Place the ruler over the edge of the fabric, lining up the appropriate measured line with the cut edge of the fabric, and then roll the cutter.

Tip

With some fabrics, the grid lines on the mat can be distracting. You can turn the mat over and cut on the other side.

Look before You Cut

If you always cut fabric following the horizontal grain line, *stop*. A lot of fabric is printed directionally and off-grain. It is important to **cut following print lines. This is true for strips, patches, and especially for sashes, borders, and bindings, where crooked prints can give the illusion of badly cut or matched fabrics,** even when they are cut perfectly straight. Borders are often cut on the lengthwise grain so they can be seamless; the stability of the straight grain also helps to eliminate wavy edges.

Tip

If you have a fabric that is printed off-grain, make your cut with a single layer of fabric to ensure that your cut follows the print and the strips will not look askew.

Quilting "Rules" to Live By

Press, Don't Iron

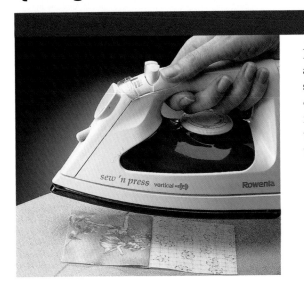

Never iron: *press*. **Move the iron up and down, rather than from side to side,** which will push the fabric piece out of shape. When you do move the iron slightly, always try to go with the grain; never move at an angle to the weave of the threads.

Press as You Go

Press the units of your block as they are constructed. If a block has many intersecting seams, it is much simpler to press them as you go, rather than to wait and press them all at the end, when the iron may force some areas in the wrong direction. Pressing as you go also makes assembling units easier.

Look before You Press

If you begin to press your block without paying attention to the seam allowances, *stop*. The direction the seam allowances are pressed can seriously affect the final look of your quilt. A general rule is to press them to the dark fabric. **However, if your quilting plan calls for quilting-in-the-ditch, it is a good idea to grade the seams and press them away from the background, regardless of its color.** If you have a block with very sharp points, sew the patches together with a shortened stitch length. The tight machine stitching will allow you to press the seams open where the points meet, making for nice, crisp points.

Go Easy on Your Blocks

If you've completed your block and are giving it a final press, *don't* drag the iron. Many perfect blocks are distorted by careless pressing. Use the iron in an up-and-down motion, first finger-pressing seams in the directions you have chosen. **Consider a shot of spray sizing or starch to give firmness to the block.**

Tip

Use a ruler to make sure your block is square before giving it that final press. See the tips on page 51 if it's not.

Clotheslines Are Nice, But . . .

Never dry a wet quilt over a clothesline. The weight of the wet quilt, two layers of fabric plus batting, will drag the lower edge of the quilt out of shape. In addition, the extra weight may even pop some quilting stitches. When all the excess water is pressed out of the quilt, lay it outside on a clean sheet to dry. Place another clean sheet over the top to protect it from birds and other creatures. Outside, on a deck in the shade is a perfect place. Avoid direct sunlight. **In the house, on a sheet over a carpet with a fan running is an acceptable alternative.**

Avoid Blurry Photos

If your photo transfer is blurred and fuzzy, the thread count of the fabric you are using may be too low. **Pima cotton, with a high thread count, will produce the smoothest image, whether transferring photographs or doing fabric painting.** Test the many different methods and products currently available for transferring photographs, and use the finest cotton fabric you can find.

End at the Point

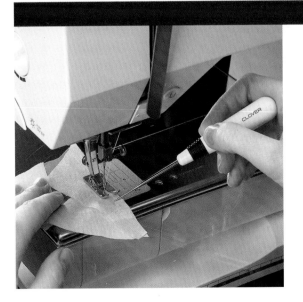

If you are piecing long, skinny points, as in a Mariner's Compass, don't start stitching at the skinny point. **Begin sewing at a wider point if possible, stitching into the sharp point. You can control the seam and the point for the last couple of inches with a stiletto (also called an awl),** keeping the fabric flat and the point lined up.

Dynamite Tips
from the Pros

Take a class from a good quilting teacher, and chances are you'll learn a great deal more than you anticipated. That's because teachers are always slipping in extra tips and tidbits of information during their classes. These pearls of wisdom are often worth their weight in gold, even though they may seem ordinary or commonplace on the surface. We asked several teachers for their favorite tips. Here we offer some that these professional quilting teachers say always elicit oohs and aahs of appreciation from their students.

Tips from the Professionals

Dot-to-Dot Color Strategy

Mimi Dietrich says lightbulbs go on for her students when she tells them about this fun and easy way to select fabrics. Look at a multicolor fabric that you love. Very often there are small dots of color printed along one selvage edge. The manufacturer uses these dots to select and position the colors on a printed fabric. Quilters can use them to help select coordinating fabrics for a quilt. **Cut a swatch of the fabric including the dots, and keep it in your purse when you shop. Match fabrics to the dots to help you make the choices for your next quilt.**

Pillow Power

Mimi Dietrich suggests that you find a firm pillow to place in your lap while you appliqué. Rest your hands on the pillow as you stitch or do handwork. The pillow will provide support for your wrists, arms, and shoulders. You will find yourself sitting up straighter, and the work will be closer to your eyes. As a bonus, the pillow can also be used as a big pincushion.

Controlling Wayward Threads

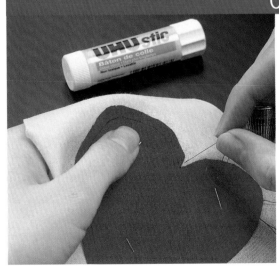

Here's another of Mimi Dietrich's favorite tricks for hand appliqué. Control fraying threads at inside points by using a little glue stick on your needle. Move your needle over the top of the glue stick, getting just a little glue on the tip of your needle. Quickly sweep the needle between the seam allowance and the background fabric, tucking any frayed threads behind the appliqué piece. The little dab of glue from the needle will transfer to the seam allowance and hold the frayed edges in place while you sew them down securely.

Freezer Paper for Appliquéd Curves

Mimi Dietrich loves to baste fabric pieces over freezer paper when she appliqués. Baste through the appliqué, the paper, and the seam allowance. When there is a sharp curve, however, change the technique slightly. **As you get near the curve, baste through the seam allowance only, keeping the running stitches very small and near the cut edge.** As you finish the curve, stitch through the paper again to secure the stitches, then gently pull on the basting thread. The fabric will pull over the edge of the curve, and the small stitches will make small, even gathers, creating a smooth edge on the appliquéd curve.

Window Template for Dimensional Appliqué

The price for having Plexiglas cut can vary considerably, so make some phone calls first to determine the cost.

It can be difficult to trim and square dimensional appliqué blocks because a ruler will not lie flat on top of them. **Karen Kay Buckley suggests you have a framing or glass-cutting shop cut a window template from mat board or Plexiglas.** The opening should include the seam allowance. If you want a 14-inch finished block, have the opening cut to 14½ inches. Center the opening over your block, measure to be sure it is centered, and draw the lines on all four sides of the opening. Use a ruler, mat, and rotary cutter to trim the block on the lines you drew.

Cutting Squares & Rectangles

If you have numerous squares and rectangles to cut and are someone who sometimes uses the wrong line on your ruler, Sharyn Craig suggests making a tape guide for foolproof cutting. Take a piece of ¼-inch masking tape and position it along one of the lines on your ruler. **With a pen or pencil, mark and label the increments according to the measurements you need to cut. Just position the strip under the ruler and place the number at the end of the strip.** If you're cutting several different sizes from the same strip, move the ruler down and cut the various pieces.

Sewing Corner to Corner

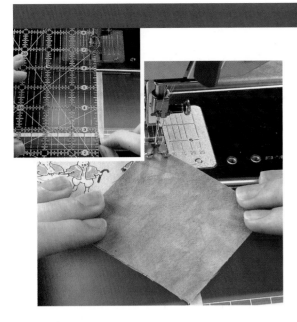

Sharyn Craig has an easy way to sew a perfect diagonal from corner to corner. Drop your needle into the bobbin area. **Position a ruler gently up against the left edge of the needle. Lower the presser foot. Position a piece of masking tape along the right edge of the ruler.** The left edge of the tape and the needle now line up. Position the units to be sewn under the presser foot so the needle starts at a corner. The opposite corner lines up on the left edge of the tape. **As you sew, keep that corner lined up with the tape.**

The Bias Controversy

Jane Hall likes to stress to her students that it is not always necessary to stitch a bias edge to a straight edge. **It is much more important to maintain the integrity of the grain line or the print line in the fabric.** Forget the old dictum that you must never stitch a bias edge to a bias edge. Too often that leads to tipped grain in some patches. Orient templates on the fabric as they appear in the block pattern and handle the cut patches with care to avoid stretching.

Trouble-Free Triangle Squares

Many times you need several triangles of the same two fabrics sewn together to make a square. Add ⅞ inch to the finished size of the triangle square to determine the size of the square; then cut the square in half on the diagonal. **Karen Kay Buckley saves a lot of time and improves her accuracy by placing the two fabrics that will be sewn together with right sides together before cutting.** Cut as usual, and the two fabrics are already right sides together. Simply pick up the triangle pairs and sew them together.

Tip

If the finished size of your square measures 2 inches, cut your square 2⅞ inches before cutting it in half diagonally.

Clip & Blunt

You've rotary cut your triangles without a template, you've chain pieced them together, and you are now ready to clip them apart. Sharyn Craig gives you another way to save yourself a considerable amount of time. **Clip the units apart and blunt the triangle (also called cutting off the dog ears) in the same motion.** If you don't know what direction to angle your scissors at for the blunting, then first open one of the units and press the seam allowance. Clip the ears. Close the unit up again and see what angle was created. For the rest of the units you need only mimic that angle.

Unit Clipper

Sharyn Craig learned this hint from one of her students. She thinks it is one of the slickest tricks she's come across in a long time. **Take the seam ripper that came with your sewing machine and insert the handle into the hole of a spool of thread. To clip your chain of sewn pieces apart, simply position the threads between units across the "valley" in the seam ripper.** Just like that, the units are apart. Continue down the chain of pieces.

Quilting Embellished Quilts

Mary Stori prefers to quilt in a hoop or small frame to maintain the proper tension of the fabric layers. Embellishments such as beads will prevent the top wooden hoop or plastic clips from being secured onto the frame. Rather than damaging the embellishments or struggling to hold the quilt layers by hand, she has a wonderful solution.

Lay the quilt over the bottom hoop or frame. Using your hands, fold the quilt around the edges and just under the bottom edge of the hoop. **Secure the quilt layers together around the hoop using small safety pins. Adjust the placement of the pins to provide the appropriate amount of tension.**

Baste before Binding

Before you apply the binding to your quilt, Mimi Dietrich recommends that you baste around the edge of your quilt. If you are afraid that the finished edge will ripple, gently pull the basting thread until the edge of the quilt is the measurement you desire. Ease any fabric gathers along the thread to smooth out the edge and distribute the fullness. The basting thread will stabilize the edge of your quilt while you apply the binding.

Machine-Stitched Quilt Labels

Quilters have become educated about the importance of documenting our quilts, and quilters use many methods to create labels. **Mary Stori uses the programmable alphabet on her computerized sewing machine to quickly achieve professional-looking labels.** Stabilize the fabric prior to sewing to allow the stitches to form accurately and prevent the cloth from tunneling. Removing some tear-away stabilizers can distort the stitching, so Mary shares her trick below for creating successful labels.

Tip

Mark a few reference lines with a removable marking pencil, to keep the stitching straight.

Stabilizing Fabric for Stitching

Here's Mary Stori's trick to create a stable fabric for machine stitching. First, select the fabric you want to use for the label. Cut it about two inches larger than the desired finished size. Secure it to a wire clothes hanger using safety pins or clothespins, and hang it outside or over a sink or laundry tub. *Saturate* **the fabric with heavy-duty spray starch, and let it air dry. It should be very stiff.** If it's not, repeat the spray process. Press flat. After completing the stitching, wash out the starch, press dry, and cut to the appropriate measurement.

DYNAMITE TIPS FROM THE PROS

Sidestepping a Quilter's
Pet Peeves

Every quilter has a pet peeve, and every cat loves quilts. While there's not a whole lot we can suggest to keep your cats off your quilts, there are a few things you can do to sidestep other pet peeves. Living in a time when so many people are quilters is great because quilters love to share, and sharing tips about overcoming pet peeves is at the top of their list. The ideas in this chapter were written by quilter and author Janet Wickell, and they may help you work through some of the annoying little things that seem to affect us all at one time or another.

Tackling the Tough Stuff

Tangled Bias Stems

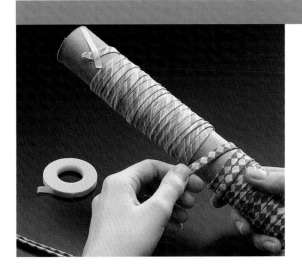

Narrow bias tubes are often used for appliqué stems, stained glass quilts, and Celtic appliqué. If you have just a few short pieces of bias tubing, organization isn't usually a problem. But storing tubes of several widths and lengths can result in a tangled mess. **To keep them nicely pressed and tangle-free, wrap sewn and pressed bias tubes around empty paper towel or bathroom tissue rolls. Use a bit of masking tape on the ends to keep them in place, and unroll the length you need as you work.**

Clinging or Scorched Bits of Freezer Paper

Freezer paper is a handy item for doing appliqué and piecing templates. Use a dry iron on the medium setting when pressing it onto fabric, and press just long enough for the paper to adhere—no more than a second or two. **If little bits of paper and plastic are hard to remove later, use an iron placed slightly above the fabric and deliver a few shots of steam to the area. Then gently pull the residue away while it is still moist. If that doesn't work, try tweezers to extract bits of paper, or use a spray bottle to moisten the paper with cool water.** Cloth stretches more easily when it is wet, so work carefully to avoid stretching patches out of shape.

Thread Breaks when Ending a Line of Quilting

Popping a knot through the fabric so it lodges between a quilt top and the batting is an effective way to end a line of quilting stitches. If you tug on it a bit too hard, though, the knot can snap, leaving a tiny tail of thread that's impossible to bury inside the layers of the quilt. When this happens, **use a pair of tweezers to gently "unquilt" several stitches, leaving a longer tail of thread.** Then wrap it around the needle again, and pop another knot through the quilt top.

Tip

Sometimes it's easier to take your needle to the back of the quilt and pop the knot through the backing fabric, avoiding seam allowances.

Visible Thread Tails

Thread that exactly matches the color of an appliqué piece makes appliqué stitches blend into the fabric almost invisibly. Sometimes, though, dark thread tails can stray and show through a light or sheer background fabric. **When that happens, use a delicate steel crochet hook to pull the tails out of sight without leaving a large hole in the background fabric. A size 14 hook works well.**

Fusible Adhesive Sticks to Ironing Board

Tip

Add a layer of parchment paper on top of your fabrics, too, to keep fusibles from sticking to the bottom of your iron.

No matter how careful you are, it's easy to get fusible adhesive stuck to your ironing board cover. **The next time you do some fusible appliqué, protect the ironing board with a piece of cooking parchment paper.**

Machine Quilting Leaves Large Needle Holes

Tip

For quilts containing synthetic fabrics (which don't relax as natural fibers do) or fabrics that can't be dampened, try using a finer machine needle and thread.

Machine quilting can sometimes leave noticeable needle holes in a quilt. **To close these holes, spritz the area with cool water.** Moisture gives cotton fibers an opportunity to relax, and as they do, they fill in holes left by the needle going through the quilt.

Freezer Paper Appliqué for Little Patches

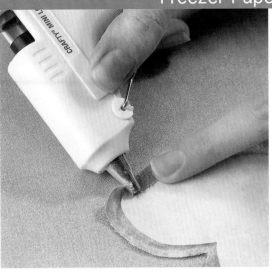

Freezer paper makes great appliqué templates, but it can often be difficult to manipulate the bulky tip of an iron around the corners and edges of small pieces. **A hot glue gun (with no glue stick!) is the answer. Its small tip and easy-to-hold handle make it a breeze to press seam allowances onto freezer paper and create perfect points and smooth curves.** For best results, use a high-temperature glue gun.

Tip

To avoid getting glue residue on fabric, purchase a new glue gun and reserve it for appliqué projects.

Evenly Spaced Quilting Stitches

The more quilting experience you gain, the more evenly spaced your quilting stitches will become. To become accustomed to taking even stitches, try using Tiger Tape. This reusable masking tape is made just for quilters, with printed lines that indicate 9 or 12 stitches per inch. **Just place the tape along the lines you want to quilt, and follow the marks as you go—your stitches will be uniform and lovely.**

Tip

After you've finished a line of quilting stitches, remove the strip of Tiger Tape and reuse it for another line of stitches.

Pin-Pricked Fingers from Sewing Binding

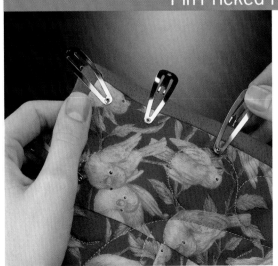

Rather than using straight pins to secure the binding in position for hand sewing, try binding clips. These curved little clips resemble hair barrettes, and they will hold binding firmly in place while you blind stitch around a quilt. There are no sharp points to prick you, and the clips can be snapped open and shut quickly and easily to remove or adjust them as you work.

Tangled Threads

Tip

If you don't have beeswax, try Thread Heaven, a silicone conditioner that smoothes out thread without leaving any waxy residue. (See the tip on page 29.)

If your thread becomes tangled, frayed, or knotted while you quilt or appliqué, try pulling it through a cake of beeswax before you begin to stitch. Beeswax will hold the thread fibers together and help it glide more easily through the fabric. You can remove any excess beeswax by sliding a thumbnail and finger down the length of the thread before you start sewing. Or place the waxed thread between two paper towels and press it with an iron.

Bearding on Quilts

Tip

Closely spaced quilting motifs help prevent bearding, too, because the more quilting stitches there are, the more the fibers will stay securely in place.

Bearding occurs when batting migrates through fabric and onto the surface of a quilt, leaving a fuzzy white coating that resembles a soft beard. Synthetic fibers are more likely to beard than cotton or wool, so if you prefer a synthetic batt, choose one that has been bonded, a process that helps keep a batt's fibers intact. Avoid using loosely woven fabrics in your quilt. High-quality, tightly woven fabric makes it harder for batting fibers to migrate. To remove bearding, rub a damp washcloth across the surface of the quilt or use a fabric shaver. See "Clean Is Nice" on page 104.

Bearding Revisited

To avoid annoying white bearding on a quilt made primarily of dark fabrics, consider using a dark batting. There are black polyester battings available, and a wonderful dark wool batting that is incredibly soft and warm. See "Quilter's Marketplace" on page 124.

Thread Unwinds from Spools

It's wonderful to accumulate a large selection of colorful threads for piecing, appliquéing, and quilting, but if the tails from all of those spools get tangled, an incredible mess is the result. **A variety of inexpensive options are available commercially, including Thread Maids, which slip into spools to hold thread tails in place. Little pink plastic Bobbin Buddies will keep your filled bobbins organized and neat.** Check your local quilt shop for these handy little gems.

Burned Fingers with Freezer Paper Appliqué

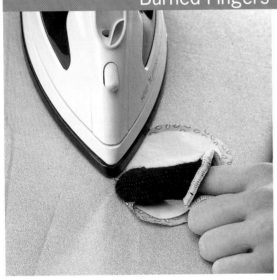

Freezer paper appliqué is a great technique, but it's easy to end up with singed fingers if they get a bit too close to the iron. **A finger protector is an inexpensive way to avoid burns.** These commercially made finger wraps are made from a non-heat-conducting material, so you can get as close to the iron as you wish and still keep your fingers cool. They are available at quilt shops.

Squaring-Up Large Blocks

Making sure that blocks are truly square is one of the best ways to make sure a quilt top will go together easily and turn out smooth and flat. **You can use one of the many different quilter's square rulers now available in sizes ranging from 6 inches all the way up to 15 and 16½ inches square.** Trim larger blocks with a 6 × 24-inch ruler butted up against your largest square ruler.

Quilter's
Time-Shavers

Want to find more quilting time? Rethinking your working methods is a great way to gain time and, not so incidentally, perhaps improve your skills in the process. In this chapter, Dixie Haywood, award-winning quilter, author, and teacher, suggests that you explore each step in the process of quiltmaking. See if there is a better way to do it by using new techniques, new tools, or by more efficiently organizing the tasks to be done.

Timely Tips

Use a Rotary Cutter with Templates

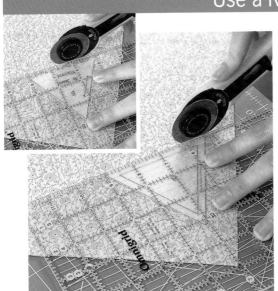

When you need to cut with templates, use a rotary cutter instead of scissors to save marking and cutting time. **Position finished-size templates with straight edges directly on the fabric with a ruler extending ¼ inch beyond the edge of the template** to add the seam allowance as the piece is cut. **To use a template with the seam allowance included, position the edge of the ruler on the edge of the template.** Hold templates in place by using double-faced tape or adhesive sandpaper dots on the back. Or, brush rubber cement on the template back and let it dry.

Spray the template back with a temporary adhesive to make it slip-proof.

Set Up an Assembly Line

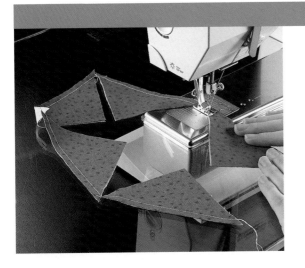

When piecing the blocks for a quilt, use assembly line techniques. Pin or stack the first two pieces for all the blocks, chain piece them through the machine, cut them apart, and press. Repeat the process for the next step in the block. This is much faster than making each block separately. It also helps keep the blocks a consistent size; individually pieced blocks have more opportunities for piecing variations.

Make a sample block first to test that the pieces are cut correctly and to use as a model.

Bias Stems Using the Roll-Over Method

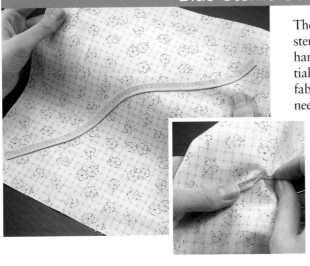

The roll-over method of sewing bias stems makes narrow stems easy to handle and appliqué, since you are initially working with a wider strip of fabric. Cut a bias strip the length needed and ¾ inch wide. This will result in a stem ⅛ inch wide; adjust the cutting width for a thicker stem. Press in half lengthwise. **Sew the folded strip in position with a running stitch and ¼-inch seam allowance, measuring from the raw edge. Roll the folded edge over the seam allowance, trimming it as necessary to contain it within the stem.**

To save more time on a long stem, do the initial stitching by machine.

Store Supplies where They Are Used

Tip

For quick pressing or trimming as you sew, open a drawer of your sewing machine cabinet and put a Quilter's Cut 'n Press board across it.

Avoid toting supplies from place to place by storing them where they are used, duplicating supplies you use regularly in more than one place. Having the proper supplies at hand will allow you to take advantage of spare moments to work rather than waste time tracking down what you need.

Cut Ahead for Binding & Hanging

Tip

Stitch the top of the sleeve to the quilt as you apply the binding if the sleeve is to be permanent.

Don't put your fabric away until you have cut the binding and a hanging sleeve (if the quilt will be hung). This will save you from digging fabric and thread out later for these finishing steps. **Sew and press the binding strips as you piece the quilt, then label and store them until you are ready for them.** Make a sleeve when you are cutting and piecing the back, making it about 2 inches shorter than the quilt width to allow for quilting take-up. Making the sleeve from the backing fabric makes it unobtrusive and gives your quilt a quality touch.

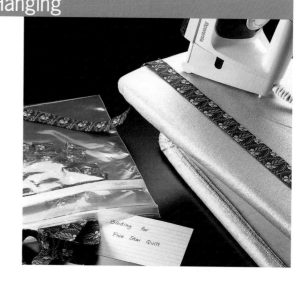

An Oversize Pressing Surface

Tip

Fasten removable or folding legs to the board for fast and easy setup and takedown.

Save time repositioning fabric and have distortion-free pressing by making or purchasing an oversize pressing surface. To make your own, cut a piece of plywood the size of your cutting surface or tabletop. Stretch an old wool blanket taut over the edge of the plywood, and staple it to the wrong side. Repeat with a layer of muslin, gridded canvas, or silver heat-reflective fabric. When not in use, store the pressing board against a wall or under a bed. Perfect Press (from Nancy's Notions) is a 23 × 62-inch cushioned pressing cloth made specifically to fit over plywood. (See also Big Board tip on page 23.)

Speed up the Basting Process

Get quilting faster with one of these three ways to speed up the basting process. The first, pin basting, is done with nickel-plated safety pins, either straight or curved. Using a quilt basting gun and a plastic grid is even faster. Both pins and tacks should be placed every 3 inches to avoid shifting of the layers. For the quickest job of all, use quilt basting spray. This ozone-friendly product is sprayed on the wrong sides of both the quilt top and backing before layering them with the batting. The spray is acid-free and washes out completely. (See "Basting Spray" on page 30.)

(See "Basting Spray" on page 30.)

Use a Kwik Clip or grapefruit spoon to make closing pins easier.

Time-Shaving Labels

Label your quilt with preprinted labels, or make your own quickly and easily with stencils, stamps, a typewriter, or your computer. A variety of preprinted labels and stencils, with appropriate art, is available. (See "Quilter's Marketplace" on page 124.) It's fun to make your own using a typewriter or computer. Iron freezer paper to starched muslin or other light-color fabric to make it easy to feed into a typewriter, inkjet printer, laser printer, or some dot matrix printers. Let the ink dry for a day before heat-setting it with a dry iron.

(See "Quilter's Marketplace" on page 124.)

Use Precut Bias

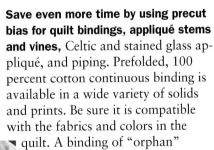

Save even more time by using precut bias for quilt bindings, appliqué stems and vines, Celtic and stained glass appliqué, and piping. Prefolded, 100 percent cotton continuous binding is available in a wide variety of solids and prints. Be sure it is compatible with the fabrics and colors in the quilt. A binding of "orphan" fabric may look out of place on a quilt made of only a few fabrics.

Be sure the batting you are using will fill the binding. With a thinner batting you may need to trim the binding or use a slightly larger seam allowance.

Always use 100% cotton binding. Cotton blend binding will not look right with the 100% cotton fabrics in a quilt.

QUILTER'S TIME-SHAVERS

Aches
& Pains

Quilting isn't exactly a contact sport, but any activity with repetitive motion puts stress on your body and can lead to aches and pains. Hours spent at the sewing machine, at the quilting frame, or pushing a needle take their toll. The way to avoid discomfort may be buying new equipment or finding new ways of working with what you have. It always means paying attention to your body. Dixie Haywood, teacher, author, and award-winning quilter, points the way to pain-free quilting.

Quilters' Comforts

Having an adjustable chair at your sewing machine isn't a luxury; it's an investment in your body's well-being. "Try on" secretarial chairs to find one that fits; one size does *not* fit all. Look for a five-leg base for stability and quality casters to make movement easy. **Adjust the height so your hands are on the bed of your sewing machine when your arms are bent at a 90 degree angle and your feet are flat on the floor.** Adjust the back. If your sewing machine bed is higher or lower than 29 to 30 inches, you may need to adjust the table.

Lean from the Waist

When working at the machine or the quilt frame, lean forward from the waist rather than bending the neck and hunching the shoulder. It will keep your back in proper alignment and enable you to work without strain.

Tilt Your Machine

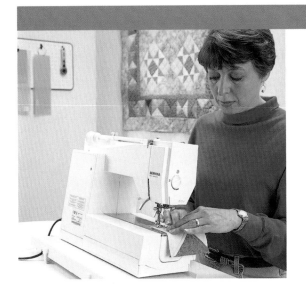

Tilting your machine can give you a better view of your needle and relieve back, neck, and eye strain. Try different angles to see which works for you. If you find it helps, you can invest in a commercial product called Tilt'able, which is available at quilt shows (or see "Quilter's Marketplace" on page 124 for ordering information). The Tilt'able was designed by a chiropractor for professional seamstresses who were suffering back and neck problems from long hours spent at the sewing machine.

ACHES & PAINS

91

Control Your Foot Pedal & Balance Your Feet

Avoid strain on your back, hips, knees, and feet by stabilizing the foot pedal under your machine. A nonslip mat will keep it in place. A slanted base will put your foot at a comfortable angle for sustained sewing. Balance the other foot at the same height with a piece of Styrofoam, wood, or one of the commercial foot pedal systems, such as the Tilt'able Sure Foot system. See "Quilter's Marketplace" on page 124.

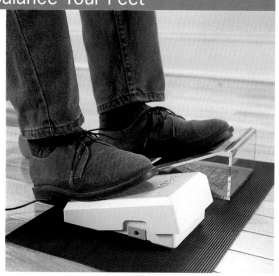

Keep Balanced with Weights

Back weights, such as the Body Rite, encourage good posture and counterbalance your back when you are working with your hands in front of you. This is useful while rotary cutting, sewing at the machine, quilting at a frame, or using the computer. See "Quilters Marketplace" on page 124.

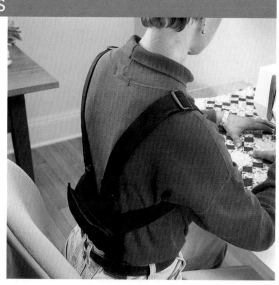

Avoid Eyestrain at the Machine

To see *exactly* where to start and stop stitching, attach a magnifier to your machine. Several types of magnifiers are available for the machine that help you see better and do not distort what you're looking at. Some, such as this enlarger/magnifier light, have built-in lighting as an added feature. See "Quilter's Marketplace" on page 124.

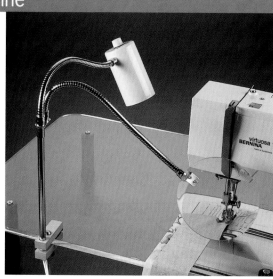

Avoid Eyestrain when Hand Stitching

Good lighting for quilting or appliquéing should come over the left shoulder if you are right handed, or over the right shoulder if you work with your left hand. This avoids throwing a shadow across your work. **If you need a close-up light, try one that you wear around your neck; it's great for quilting dark fabric with dark thread. If you need magnification as well, there are magnifiers to wear around your neck or on your head,** and there are many lamps with built-in magnifiers.

Prevent Pricked Fingers

Avoid pricked and sore fingers on the hand under the quilt by using a finger protector. Some protectors are worn like a thimble, one kind is held in your hand, and others wrap around your finger. Some also help form the stitch by guiding the needle upward. You can raid the kitchen and use a canapé knife or infant spoon for a protector and needle guide; hold it in your hand and guide it with your thumb. All of these take a little time and practice to get used to, but they do work. See also "T.J.'s Quick Quilter" tip on page 29.

Treating Pricked Fingers

If one finger becomes too sore for comfort, use another while it heals. **Keep a styptic pencil handy to stop bleeding and soreness from needle pricks. Try coating your quilting fingers with clear nail polish to cushion them against pricks. Some quilters also use products such as New-Skin (available in drug stores) to protect sore fingers.**

Tip

Reduce stress on your fingers and hands by using a needle grabber when quilting through bulky seams.

A C H E S   &   P A I N S

93

Cushion Your Legs & Feet

Position cushioned mats on the floor at the cutting table and ironing board; your legs and feet will thank you. These mats are often used in kitchens and restaurants to alleviate fatigue from standing for long periods of time. Look for them at home supply stores. For heavy-duty cushioning, check with a professional kitchen supply store.

Raise Your Cutting Table

Tip

Use your kitchen counter as a marking and cutting surface.

If your cutting surface is normal table height, it is probably too low. Depending on how tall you are, the ideal cutting surface is closer to the height of a kitchen counter. For rotary cutting, the surface should be 6 to 8 inches below your elbow. **Raise a too-low table by setting the legs on blocks of wood or other stable risers.**

Take Care of Your Wrist

Tip

Always keep the blades on your scissors and rotary cutter sharp. This will reduce pressure on your hand and wrist when cutting.

Carpal tunnel syndrome seems to be epidemic among quilters. **To help avoid the problem, explore ergonomically designed scissors and rotary cutters to see if they are easier and more comfortable to use.** Keep your wrist as straight as possible when rotary cutting and hand quilting. Use your elbow and shoulder to help move and to reduce stress on your wrist, and learn to cut with either hand, if possible. **If you're already feeling twinges in your wrists, try Lycra gloves or wristbands for relief from pain and cramping.** See "Quilter's Marketplace" on page 124.

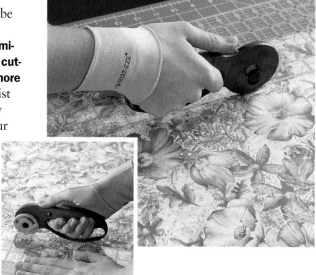

94

Pay Attention to Your Body

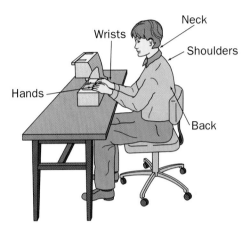

Neck
Wrists
Shoulders
Hands
Back

The best way to avoid aches and pains is to balance your workload and pace yourself. Check your posture when sitting or standing, and become aware of what muscles are being used for different tasks. Alternate large muscle and small muscle activities, and take breaks often. Working those extra minutes (or hours) is counterproductive if it puts your body at risk.

Quilter Tristan Mor shares the minibreak routine that she received from the Tallahassee Memorial Hospital Outpatient Rehabilitation Unit.

Use the following 3-minute routine at least every 2 hours while engaged in sitting activities. Perform each exercise for 20 seconds. Do the first seven steps while sitting. It's best to check with your doctor before trying this stretching regime.

1. Inhale slowly through your nose, and gently exhale through your mouth.
2. Drop your ear toward your shoulder; repeat on the other side.
3. Make circles with your shoulders by shrugging them up to your ears, pulling them back, and dropping them down.
4. Rotate your ankles in circles to pump blood back up to your brain.
5. Place your hands on your hips, and increase and decrease the curve of your lower back.
6. Drop your head to your knees, and rub the muscles in your lower back.
7. Place your hands on the seat of your chair on either side of your hips. Push down and attempt to lift your body weight from the chair.
8. Stand, support your lower back with your hands, and gently arch backwards.
9. Stand with your back flat against the wall and gently slide down the wall 4 to 5 inches, bending your knees. Count to three and stand.
10. Sit down. Concentrate on sitting up straight! Pull your head back, up, and in to keep it aligned with your spine.

Warning Signs of Repetitive Strain Injuries
The following warning signs should not be ignored if they persist. Damage can be serious and permanent, if left untreated:

❏ Tightness, stiffness, soreness, or burning sensations in hands, wrists, fingers, arms, or elbows.
❏ Numbness, tingling, or coldness in hands.
❏ Loss of strength or coordination in hands.

ACHES & PAINS

The Traveling
Quilter

Yes, you can take it with you! Whether you're waiting for appointments, going on vacation, or traveling to a quilt conference, you can continue working on your quilt. Dixie Haywood—veteran traveling quilter, teacher, and author—has gathered some super tips to take advantage of time, and to make quilting and globe-trotting good travel companions.

Quilting on the Go

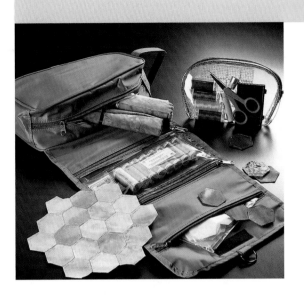

Keep a tote bag packed with basic supplies. A see-through cosmetic bag makes it easy to locate what you need and is strong enough not be punctured easily. This makes it convenient for local spur-of-the-moment trips when you know you will have waiting time.

Always have a small handwork project available to pick up and carry with you to work on in meetings, while waiting for appointments, or while visiting. Make it easy to pick up as you walk out the door. You'll be surprised by how much you can get done in spare moments.

Working in a Confined Space

When working in a confined public space, such as an office, waiting room, or airplane, keep your work and your tools compact. **A chatelaine that secures scissors, threads, needles, pins, and a thimble around your neck is a good way to manage your tools.** It can be as simple as a ribbon with the end folded and stitched into a thimble pocket and a tie to attach scissors and thread. Or make it as elaborate and creative as you like with your own imagination or a purchased pattern. A clip-on Zinger with a retractable cord to hold a small pair of scissors is another handy travel accessory.

Tip

Use a "wooden iron"—a small wooden gadget with a flat, angled side—to press short seams or to turn under seam allowances.

Use a Travel Desk

On an airplane you can use the fold-down tray on the seat back in front of you for a work space. In an automobile or while waiting at the airport, **a travel or lap desk with a beanbag-type bottom and a hard top will serve as a great portable work surface.** Most are small enough to tuck into a tote bag with your project.

Tip

Thread several needles before you leave. If the ride is bumpy, you won't have to struggle to get the thread into that teeny hole.

THE TRAVELING QUILTER

Precut Fabric

Tip

For space-effective packing, take a travel iron and a soft ironing pad that can be rolled.

Plan to cut your fabric before you leave. Cutting fabric prior to going on a trip saves having to carry bulky supplies and cutting tools. **Store the fabric in plastic zipper bags according to shape or color. Keep bags together by punching holes in the top and putting them on a key ring or a large safety pin.**

Think Thread

If you are working with a variety of fabrics, perhaps a neutral thread will blend with them all. If not, or if you are doing appliqué, **wind some thread of each color you need around a piece of cardboard. Make a notch near each thread to hold the thread end securely in place.**

Spill-Proof Pins

Make a spill-proof pin holder to take with you when you're on the go. Cut two 3-inch cardboard circles and two 3½-inch circles of fabric. **Wrap the fabric over the edge of each cardboard circle, and glue the seam allowance in place with fabric glue spread around the edge of the cardboard.** If desired, glue a hanger of folded ribbon to the inside of one of the pieces. With wrong sides together, whipstitch the two fabric-covered circles together. **Insert pins around the circle so that they are secure between the pieces of cardboard.** Glass-head pins are easiest to remove and provide a decorative edge.

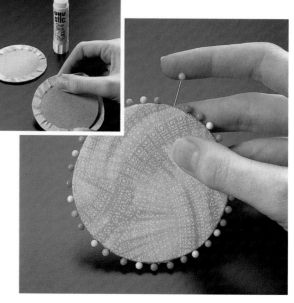

When packing cutters, protect the blades with covers or cases so they don't poke through fabric and other supplies as they are jostled. Use an old eyeglass case for rotary cutters, or purchase a blade guard, available from quilt shops and mail order catalogs. It's amazing how rotary cutters almost always work themselves open during long airplane flights. It's also a good idea to transport scissors with their protective blade covers.

Make a Block Carrier Book

Keep patches of fabric for pieced or appliquéd blocks in place, and provide storage for finished blocks with a block carrier book. Cut 6 to 8 pieces of cotton flannel and a piece of upholstery-weight fabric 14 × 28 inches with pinking sheers or a deckle-edged rotary cutter. If you have a serger, you can serge the edges. Lay the upholstery fabric wrong side up with the flannel pieces on top. Sew through the middle to make 14-inch-square "pages." Fold a 24-inch ribbon in half and sew it to the back cover for a tie. Lay the pieces for each block on a separate page, **roll, and tie closed.**

A Portable Quilt Frame

A convenient frame for the traveling quilter is a Q-Snap frame that can be taken apart for packing and easily reassembled. Even a large quilt can be managed with an 11 × 17-inch frame. Pack it with the quilt so it will be readily accessible. Layer the quilt between cotton sheets and fold it to fit in a pillowcase. Be sure the quilt and pillowcase are both labeled with your name and address. Include the frame in the pillowcase, and place it in a labeled plastic bag for protection from any moisture it may encounter.

Tip

If you're working in an area that is less than pristine, drape a sheet across your lap and onto the floor to protect the quilt.

THE TRAVELING QUILTER

Keep the Quilting Thread Handy

To keep your quilting thread at hand, thread a ribbon through the spool. Loop it through a clamp on a Q-Snap frame, or tie it to the screw of a quilting hoop. It won't be lost or misplaced, and you won't have to spend time looking for your thread.

Let There Be Light

Tip

When traveling with an iron, light, or sewing machine, tuck in an extension cord. Wall outlets may not be in a convenient place.

Ensure sufficient light at workshops or in a hotel. **The lightweight tabletop Ott-Lamp gives good natural light, stays cool, and folds closed for convenient packing.** If this is more than you think you'll need, at least **pack a box of 100-watt lightbulbs to brighten a hotel lamp.**

Keeping It Together

Tip

Use adhesive address labels to identify anything you take away from home. It's easy to become distracted when packing up at a workshop or hotel.

Make or purchase a carryall that has space for mats, ironing pad and iron, fabric, and your sewing supplies. When you have a way to keep everything together, there is less chance of forgetting essentials or leaving them behind when you come home.

The Quilter's
Problem Solver

Have Sewing Machine, Will Travel

As restrictions for carry-on and checked baggage proliferate, traveling with a sewing machine takes some planning and forethought. Here are some strategies for taking your machine:

❏ If your machine will fit under the seat, it can count as one of two allowed carry-on pieces.

❏ A wheeled cart is the best way to manage a heavy machine. Be aware, however, that the cart will count as a second carry-on.

❏ If you will be checking your machine as baggage, ask a dealer for a box. Some have fitted foam padding. If it doesn't, pack it in fabric or clothing to prevent the machine from being jostled as it is handled.

❏ If you check a machine in its case, pad the inside well, and use a luggage strap to reinforce the clasp.

❏ Pack extra needles, a replacement bulb, and a three-prong adapter.

❏ If you travel with a machine frequently and don't need all the bells and whistles of your regular machine, consider purchasing a lightweight straight-stitch machine. In addition to the perennial favorite, the Singer Feather-weight, there are similar new machines.

❏ Consider renting a machine at your destination rather than taking your own. Check with quilt-show organizers if you're attending a show, or contact sewing machine shops in the town where you are going to find out where to rent a machine.

THE TRAVELING QUILTER

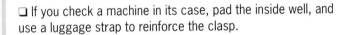
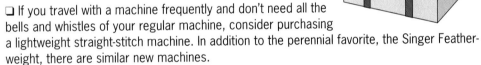

Quilt-Show *Savvy*

Everyone loves a quilt show. It is a feast for the senses; a chance to see all kinds of techniques, colors, and designs; an opportunity to meet old friends and make new ones. It is truly a quilter's dream event. How do you enter a show to have one of your quilts hanging there for the world to see? What do judges look for when they are judging quilts? How can you best survive a quilt show as a spectator? As an entrant? Read on for words of wisdom from Jane Hall, award-winning quilter and quilt-show judge who has been on all sides of the quilt-show fence.

Entering a Show

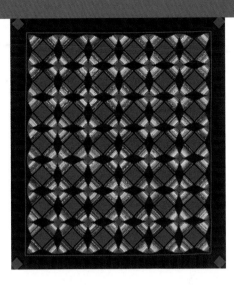

To win Best of Show is a real honor. **The Best of Show quilt is simply a very good example of the quiltmaker's art. It consists of a well-chosen, well-executed design that hangs straight without rippling or wobbling.** The Best of Show is always chosen from the blue ribbon winners by the judges. However, the Best of Show in one competition may only merit third place in another show. The judging depends on the specific show, the quilts in that show, and the judges on the panel. It is a comparison of the quilts in that particular competition.

Workmanship, Color & Design

To make a Best of Show quilt, you need to be dedicated to the mastery of your art. Your workmanship must be the best: sharp points, matching intersections, smooth curves, even stitching, straight borders, firm bindings. Take workshops, read books, and practice techniques until your skills are honed. **You must also be knowledgeable about design and color, able to produce a quilt with balance, proportion, and good color placement and values. This is true whether you are working with traditional or innovative designs.**

Details, Details, Details

Often, what makes the Best of Show is the maker's attention to detail.

• The thread color for stitching should match the fabrics in piecing and in appliqué.
• The grain line of patches and blocks should be appropriate.
• Threads and dark fabrics should not show through light areas.
• Corners should be square rather than dog-eared.
• The binding should be tight and filled with batting.

Be sure to remove all markings from construction or quilting.

Strive for Even Quilting

When you are designing the quilting pattern for your quilt, make sure that the amount of quilting is sufficient, that it enhances the design of the top, and that the quilting is evenly distributed over the surface of the quilt. **A quilt that has more quilting in some areas and not enough in others will not be in contention for Best of Show.** Exquisite stipple quilting or elegant feathers in some areas will not make up for puffy and loose areas elsewhere.

Clean Is Nice

Tip

Bearding is most noticeable on dark fabric, but it occurs with all colors and detracts from the overall appearance of an otherwise prize-winning quilt.

Be sure your quilt is clean and free from lint, fuzz, surface grime, and smoking odors. An amazing number of quilts come into shows with dirty smudges, finger-prick bloodstains, and animal hairs. Some shows eliminate these quilts from competition at the start. Clean any marks and stains, and air the quilt thoroughly. Use a lint-roller on the quilt to remove any pet hairs before you ship it. **Bearding, the migration of tiny fibers from polyester batting, can be shaved with a fabric-shaver, a battery operated device designed to remove pilling on knits.** (See also the tips on bearding on page 84.)

Let Your Quilt Go Incognito

Be sure to **attach a fabric label to the back of your quilt with your name, address, and the quilt title. Then cover your name with masking tape, or baste a piece of fabric over it.** The judges should not know who made the quilt, in order for them to be objective and impartial.

Getting Your Quilt There

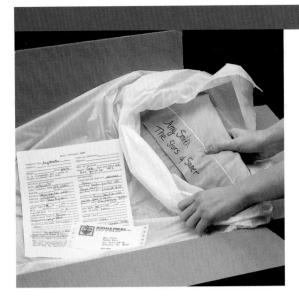

When shipping quilts to a show, many quilters prefer using private shippers such as UPS or FedEx because of their tracking systems for packages.

- Write the quilt title and your name on a pillowcase and place the quilt inside it. **Enclose the pillowcased quilt in a plastic bag.**
- Pack the quilt in a sturdy box.
- Enclose a return shipping label and postage as required. Send a check or money order only.
- Enclose a written appraisal for your quilt if its value is above the usual shipper's minimum.

Do not write "Quilt" or "Quilt Show" on the outside of the package. Use the terms "Fabric Hanging" or "Cloth Bed-cover" if necessary.

Attending a Quilt Show

Save Your Back & Shoulders

Block Party Studios in Iowa makes a collapsible tote bag on wheels that can be invaluable at a quilt show. It can hold your purse and umbrella plus all the goodies you will collect as you visit the merchants. **There is also a Healthy Back Shoulder Bag sold through several mail-order catalogs.** It comes in several sizes and will hold a lot of material without hurting shoulders by distributing weight across your back.

Quilt-Show Perks

There are many bonuses to attending quilt shows besides seeing wonderful quilts. You have access to fabric, fabric, and more fabric, and you'll find all the latest gadgets, notions, tools, and patterns. **You'll also be able to purchase goods that are not readily available elsewhere. Watch for specialty fabrics, such as hand-dyed and hand-painted fabrics, batiks, African fabrics, and screen printed originals.**

Take advantage of the opportunity to watch demonstrations of new products and try them out yourself.

QUILT-SHOW SAVVY

105

Tip

Be aware of other photographers; there may be a line waiting to shoot a particularly popular quilt.

For personal use, try a small, lightweight "point and shoot" (auto focus) camera with a built-in flash, that you can keep in your purse. Most of the quilts will be indoors and will require flash photography. **Look for a camera with a relatively fast, wide-angle lens and one that will also allow you to get close to a quilt for a detail shot (28mm or 35mm and f2.8 or f3.5).** For prints, use a 200 or 400 speed film with good color reproduction. Remember to ask permission before taking a picture of a quilt in a vendor's booth or at a demonstration.

A Quilt-Show Survival Guide

A quilt show can be the equivalent of a strenuous athletic event. Most quilt shows have vendors and the combination of looking at the quilts and attempting to visit each shop will tire even the most indefatigable. Map out a strategy that will allow you to see and do everything as leisurely as possible.

Quilt-Show Checklist:

❏ Wear comfortable shoes and socks so you can remain on your feet cheerfully for many hours. Exhibit-hall floors are often concrete and fatiguing on feet.

❏ Dress in layers of clothing, to be prepared for extremes of heat or cold.

❏ Check the layout of the show before you plunge in. Plan a route so you don't miss any part. Most people turn right when entering an exhibit; go left and avoid the crowd.

❏ Note where the bathrooms, snack bar, and seating places are. Plan your visits to avoid the rush. Either eat early or late.

❏ Carry a lightweight purse or pack, preferably over your shoulder or around your waist.

❏ Figure out how you will carry any purchases (tote bag, rolling bag, or shopping bags). Some large shows will have a package checking area where you can leave things until you are ready to depart.

❏ Bring a small camera with an extra battery and enough film. Be familiar with all the operations necessary to take your pictures.

❏ Don't attempt to see the entire show and vendor area in one long push. Take breaks for a drink or snack, and sit while you are refreshing yourself. Your senses will be overloaded, so you'll need to pace yourself.

❏ Set aside time for old and new friends, and visit both quilts and vendors in as relaxed a manner as possible.

❏ Prioritize as necessary, so that you see what you really want to see most.

The Quilter's
Problem Solver

Entering a Quilt in a Show

Submitting Slides

Large shows frequently jury first by slides to select quilts that will be judged and shown. If you are not experienced in slide photography, it is probably best to hire a professional photographer who knows how to photograph quilts. This will involve hanging them so they don't sag, using a neutral background, and using proper lighting to best reproduce the colors as well as to highlight the quilting. Have several shots taken of the whole quilt, as well as detail shots of a small area showing workmanship and fabrics up close. Project the slides on a screen in a darkened room to make sure they show the quilt exactly as you wish.

Workmanship & Design

Judges judge the entire quilt. The Show Committee decides what emphasis is to be placed on *workmanship* and on *design;* most commonly these elements are ranked equally. A judge looks at all aspects of the workmanship—the construction technique, the quilting, the finishing—noting major pluses and minuses in techniques. The design is judged with the quilt held up vertically, as the piece will be seen hung. It should elicit a positive response in all aspects, including the quilting as a design element. Many judges also note the overall appearance and presentation of a quilt as a final factor in the judging.

The Competition

No quilt is judged by itself; rather it is judged against the other quilts in the same category in that particular show. After the quilts are gone over individually, they are ranked within their category. Many times a winner in one show will not be ribboned in another. It depends entirely on the other quilts entered into the competition.

Read the Rules

Read the rules of the quilt show. Be sure you have fulfilled every one, whether it deals with size or technique or the date of making the quilt. Your quilt may be disqualified if it is not entered properly. Placing your quilt in a specific category may be difficult. Some shows have easily identified groupings, while others are more subjective.

Show & Tell

Regard a quilt show as an educational experience. If you enter with the goal of winning a prize, you will almost surely be disappointed, and you will not benefit from a wonderful learning experience. A quilt show is a hanging show-and-tell. Rarely do you have such a wonderful chance to see and compare patterns, techniques, styles, color combinations, and quilted pieces of all varieties. No two quilters will deal with a pattern or even an idea in exactly the same way. Enter a quilt show to display your quilt to your peers, to broaden your horizons by seeing all kinds of quilts, and to learn from the judges' critiques of your work.

Tips Grandma *Never Told You*

Many lucky quilters have some history of quiltmaking in the family. Grandma, Aunt Helen, or some other distant relative may be the source of quilting lore passed down. Even though what quilters do now as a matter of course is quite different from what was done 20 years ago, you can learn some new tricks by following advice from long-time quilters. Here are some time-honored tips gathered by Jane Hall, award-winning quilter and quilt-show judge. Moving a step beyond, there are also tips that Grandma might not have used, but that you *can* use and pass along.

Timeless Tips from Grandma

Use Only Good-Quality Materials

Use the best materials you can find and afford. This holds true for fabric, thread, batting, and the tools you use. There is too much time and effort spent on even a small quilt to have it be less than the best. Poor-quality fabric is more difficult to work with, can fade, and won't wear as well as top-quality goods. Poorly constructed, low-quality tools may end up costing you more in the long run by breaking and needing replacement more often. There are many things you can't control in quiltmaking—selecting high-quality materials is something you *can.*

When basting a quilt, use a neutral color or white thread, which will not leave colored lint or transfer dye onto the quilt top.

Waste Not, Want Not

String piecing is the ultimate form of fabric recycling. Use pressed-piecing, a flip-and-sew technique, to create string and crazy quilt designs on foundations of fabric or paper. **Place a piece of fabric on the foundation, right side up; the second piece on top of the first, right sides matching, and stitch through all layers. Flip the second piece of fabric open, press, and add the next piece.** Continue until the foundation is covered. Join the foundations to create blocks or units.

Tip

Even the smallest, most irregularly shaped bits of fabric can be utilized in string piecing.

Make Do

This adage has been with quilters for generations, but it is as appropriate today as it was 100 years ago. **Challenge yourself to make a quilt with what you have on hand.** (Then you can go buy something new!) Most of us can afford to *use* some of our stash, instead of just looking at it. Expand your definition of what kinds of fabrics "go together" by working within your collection and not automatically heading out the door to buy fabrics that "match." See "The Quilter's Problem Solver" on page 27 for what to do when you run out of fabric.

Things Grandma Never Heard Of

TIPS GRANDMA NEVER TOLD YOU

Freezer Paper Appliqué

Use freezer paper to keep appliqué motifs smooth and round. From freezer paper, cut the shapes exactly the finished size and **iron them onto the wrong side of the fabrics. Cut out the appliqué ³⁄₁₆ inch outside the edge of the freezer paper. Pin the shape in place on the background, and needle turn the seam allowance under, against the edge of the freezer paper.**

When you're finished stitching, cut an opening in the background fabric behind the appliqué and carefully remove the freezer paper.

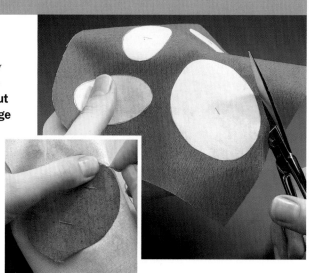

Freezer Paper Stitching Guide

Use freezer paper templates to produce precise pieced blocks. Iron finished-size freezer paper templates onto the wrong side of fabrics; cut a ¼-inch seam allowance outside the edge of the paper on all sides. **Pin the patches together, matching the cut edges of the freezer paper templates, and stitch along the edge.** You may stitch by hand or by machine, but either way, you have a marked line on which to sew, which will produce an accurate block.

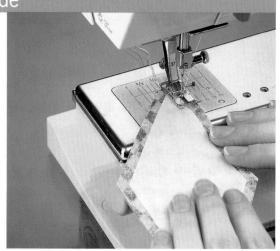

Foundations for Precise Piecing

Tip

If you want to remove the foundation, use paper. Fabric foundations remain in the quilt, adding an extra layer.

Use foundations, paper or fabric, for *any* block, not just String, Crazy, and Log Cabin designs. Draw the block on your foundation and divide it into segments, each of which can be press-pieced. **Stitch each segment, and simply join them together to make the block.** The control, stability, and precision you will gain from using foundations more than makes up for the extra steps involved.

New Gadgets, New Perspectives

When you are designing a block or a setting for blocks, borders, or sashes, **use a Polaroid camera to record different arrangements.** In addition to capturing the composition, seeing it in a snapshot gives you a slightly different view, and can help with design and color choices. **Looking at your work in a mirror, with a reducing glass, or through the wrong end of binoculars are other ways to accomplish a new view.**

A flannel-backed tablecloth or a twin-size white flannel sheet makes a wonderful design surface.

Add Quilting Supplies to Your Grocery List

Grandma may have used cocoa or cornstarch for pouncing designs on quilts, but she would probably never dream that quilters today would find so many uses for ordinary grocery items, including: **spoons for hand quilting, dryer sheets for appliqué, toothpicks for hand appliqué, cocoa and cornstarch for pouncing, dental floss and string for making a compass, freezer paper for countless uses, parchment paper for foundation piecing and machine quilting, spray starches, sizing, bleach, rubber gloves, and distilled water.**

Threading Savvy

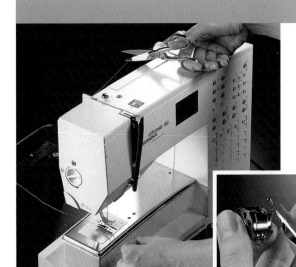

From Bernina of America, here are two up-to-date tips on unthreading your sewing machine: **First, clip the thread at the spool and pull the thread down through the needle.** This keeps the lint from being run back into the tension disks. **Second, when you change bobbins, clip the bobbin thread right at the bobbin case and drop the bobbin out.** Pulling a long tail of bobbin thread out through the slit in the bobbin case can harm the spring and cause tension problems.

If you are machine piecing several different-value fabrics, put a dark thread in the bobbin and a neutral color on the top spindle, or vice versa.

TIPS GRANDMA NEVER TOLD YOU

111

You Want Me to Piece the Back, Too?

Consider doing something special for the backing of your quilt, instead of using just one large piece of fabric. Create back art by piecing large squares or rectangles of fabric that co-ordinate with the quilt top. Use extra blocks or even piece an extra-large block of the quilt pattern for the back. **Paint or dye designs that relate to the front of the quilt. Use fabric transfers of photographs or of children's drawings.** Be mindful of the problems too many bulky seam allowances can cause, though, and try to stagger them in relation to seams from the top.

Instant Antique

Make your quilt look old on purpose. Quilt it heavily, using a cotton batting. Old quilts had a lot of quilting because the batting would migrate and lump if not held down. Then wash the quilt—use bleach to fade the fabrics, and "shock" the quilt by machine washing it with hot water and machine drying it at a hot setting. **This will shrink both fabric and batting, even if you have prewashed them, and cause puckering and softening.** You can also lay the quilt outside in the sun, but watch out for birds and stray cats!

Curing the Quilting Blahs

What do you do when a finished quilt has a case of the blahs? Use it as a painter would a canvas, and see what you can do to give it some life. **Embellish it with beads, buttons, or metallic threads. Add some appliqué. Paint new colors on the surface; overdye the entire quilt with a weak solution of red, brown, or blue. Dab a solution of half bleach and half water on specific motifs or in small areas.** Be sure to wash out excess bleach immediately. If you are not happy with your quilt, change it until you are—or give it away and start something new!

Tip

If it's still an unquilted top, try cutting it apart. Reassemble it or add new pieced segments to create something more exciting.

But It's a Perfectly Good Tie

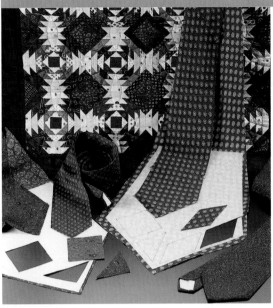

Make a wallhanging with old neckties. The colors are rich and the different textures add an exciting touch to a design. Open up the ties and remove their linings. Hand wash and rinse them, watching for bleeding. Blot excess moisture with a terry towel and air-dry until slightly damp. Press from the reverse side until completely dry. Necktie fabrics can be slippery and stretchy, but you can overcome the difficulty of working with them and combining the different weights of fabrics by stabilizing them before you cut patches. **Use lightweight fusible interfacing, which will remain in the pieces, or freezer paper if you wish to use a temporary stabilizer.**

What! You Quilt by Machine?

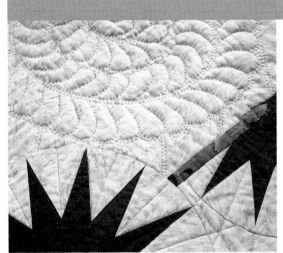

Combine hand and machine quilting in the same piece. Machine quilting produces a solid hard line, which can be a strong design element. It is extremely useful for quilting in the ditch and to enhance lines, whether in the blocks or at the borders. Hand quilting makes a soft line, with stitches separated by spaces. It is particularly appropriate for curves and feathers. Both techniques are used by themselves of course, but it is interesting to combine them in one quilt, using each to its advantage.

It's Okay to Have Bias Edges

If possible, keep the outside edges of a block on the straight or cross grain. However, **some designs, such as blocks set on point, will be better cut with bias edges on the outside. Stay stitch the edge if the fabric is particularly stretchy.** Otherwise, simply handle the patches and blocks with extra care as you assemble them.

We've all heard them, but no one seems to know exactly how they started. Maybe you heard it through the grapevine or from the notorious "quilt police." No matter what the source, we've all wondered—at least once—if what we are doing or what we have heard is "right." Sit back, relax, and join us as author and quilter Darra Williamson explodes some of the more commonly held quilting myths, legends, superstitions, and "rules." The bottom line? Choose whatever works best for you. No matter what you may have heard, *absolutely* nothing *in quiltmaking is absolute!*

You've Heard the Saying . . .

Always quilt from the center out.

You can actually start quilting *anywhere* on the quilt, if you take the time to baste properly. Smooth the three layers flat, taut, and wrinkle-free. Use sturdy, light-color thread, and take regular, medium-size basting stitches, about 1 inch long. Baste in either a grid or in a diagonal pattern, but be sure to space basting lines no more than three inches apart.

Once the layers are secure, you can quilt around blocks and rows, and then go back to fill in the details.

Tip

Some quilters actually quilt the borders first to avoid stretching them as the center of the quilt is quilted.

Amish quilters get 30 stitches to the inch.

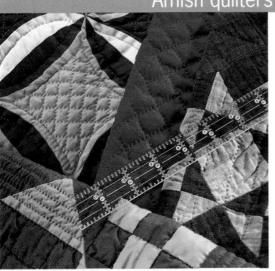

The fine stitching and elaborate motifs, particularly on antique quilts, have undoubtedly fueled this generalization about Amish quiltmakers. In truth, the Amish are just like the rest of us! Some quilt in minute, museum-quality stitches, while others produce stitches that are certainly adequate, but basically average in terms of size and number.

There is no hard and fast rule dictating how many stitches per inch constitute "good" quilting! Quilting is something to be enjoyed. It is also a skill that improves with experience.

Tip

Quilt regularly, and you'll see improvement in no time. Concentrate on stitches that are consistent in size and evenly spaced.

Vinegar or salt will stop bleeding color.

Sometimes a vinegar rinse or salt in the wash water works . . . and sometimes it doesn't. Even after repeated "treatments," some fabrics continue to release excess dye. **For a more reliable preventative, launder previously unwashed fabric in a fixative, such as Retayne, which locks the color into the fabric.**

If the quilt is finished and disaster strikes in the first washing, try Synthrapol. This product draws the excess dye from fabric (including the one stained by the "bleeder") and suspends it in the water, away from the quilt. Be sure to follow manufacturers' instructions.

QUILTING MYTHS LAID TO REST

115

Always press seam allowances to one side.

Tip

To prevent batting from creeping through the seams, set your machine to take at least 12 stitches per inch.

Actually, there are instances when it is an advantage to press seams *open*! **Multiple converging seams can be tricky when joining pieced blocks into rows or stitching rows of blocks together. By pressing these key seams open, you'll distribute the bulk more evenly.** The resulting points are crisper and more accurate, the overall quilt lies flatter, and it is easier to cross the seam lines with quilting.

Always press toward the darker fabric.

This is normally recommended to avoid shadow-through, but sometimes pressing toward the darker fabric is *not* an option. It may be impossible because of a previously stitched seam or because to do so will flip another seam in an undesirable direction. Or pressing toward the darker fabric will not permit subsequent seams to nest, or butt, for neat, accurate junctures.

Seams with shadow-through can be trimmed, graded, or even pressed open (see the preceding myth). Trust your judgement, and choose whatever works best for you and your quilt.

It will quilt out.

Tip

You'll improve accuracy and reduce frustration if you change both your rotary-cutter blade and your sewing machine needle on a regular basis.

Not necessarily! **While it is sometimes possible to tame minimal fullness in a finished quilt top, the distortion may be too great for even the most dense and masterful quilting to correct.**

Eliminate the need for "corrective quilting," by improving construction techniques. Double-check patterns, templates, and measurements for accuracy. Cut, sew, and press with care. Square-up blocks before setting the quilt top. Cut the borders to the "true" measurement of the quilt top (measured through the center) and make the top fit the border—not vice versa!

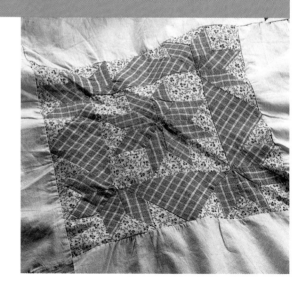

You must finish the quilting before binding.

If you piece with absolute precision, baste thoroughly and securely, and plan to distribute the quilting evenly over its entire surface, there is actually no reason why you cannot bind your quilt before quilting it. "Prebinding" a quilt can lessen the chance that the borders will stretch during the quilting process, and that the edges of the finished product will be wavy and distorted.

Tip

A line of machine basting around the perimeter of a quilt helps secure the three layers and prevents puckers and pleats when the binding is added.

Never use steam to press patches and blocks.

In reality, many irons simply do not get hot enough to press cotton blocks effectively without a bit of moisture. **A shot of steam helps eliminate wrinkles, set seams, and flatten the bulk of seam allowances for nice, crisp points.** Much of the distortion attributed to steam is actually caused by overzealous handling and ironing. Handle finished quilt blocks as little as possible. Resist the temptation to smooth them repeatedly on your design wall. Most importantly, *press* quilt blocks, don't iron them! Apply the iron with a repeated up and down, rather than back and forth, motion.

Tip

Stitching ⅛ inch from the edge around the perimeter of a finished quilt block helps prevent stretching until the block is sewn into the quilt.

Colors in a quilt must match exactly.

From a few feet away, it is usually impossible to tell if the tiny blue flower in one print is the exact shade of the polka dot in the neighboring fabric. So why obsess? Actually, these slight variations in color give a quilt much more personality than its perfectly color-coordinated sisters.

Incidentally, you are less likely to err when working with 30 fabrics than you are with three. Consider the scrap quilt, where more is definitely more! **By combining a variety of fabrics, you can explore (and blend!) *whole families* of your chosen colors, rather than struggling to find the *single* perfect shade.**

Cut so the straight grain is on the edge of the block.

Cutting pieces so that the straight grain is parallel to the edge of the block helps to maintain stability and accuracy. However, occasionally it is neither possible nor desirable. **Blocks are not always squares. Sometimes they are triangles or hexagons, making it virtually impossible to cut all outside edges along the straight grain.** Even in a square block, cutting a long inside diagonal on the straight grain simply makes more sense. When fabrics are cut to highlight a particular motif or create a special effect, grain line is not a consideration at all!

Use white or off-white thread for hand quilting.

You only need to look at the quilts of the nineteenth century to know that this is not true! Many are quilted in a variety of thread colors.

Choice of quilting thread is a matter of personal preference. Choose a colored quilting thread to add contrast or drama, or to highlight the quilting motif as an important design element. For a wonderful, old-timey flavor, try brown (chocolate, khaki, or tan) quilting thread. Experiment with rayons, silks, and metallics to add texture, interest, and an element of surprise.

Tip

A print backing fabric helps camouflage the use of different colored quilting threads on the quilt top.

Use only 100 percent cotton fabrics in your quilts.

No doubt, cotton is the preferred fabric among quiltmakers. It handles well, is durable, holds a crease, and resists pilling and fraying. But occasionally, a perfectly shaded polyester blend or some other nontraditional fabric finds its way into your scrap bag.

With careful handling and a few simple precautions, you can incorporate small amounts of nontraditional fabrics into your quilts, particularly those quilts that will not be laundered. Spray starch gives flimsy blends additional body and creasibility, while ultralight iron-on interfacing stabilizes silks, satins, and lamés.

Tip

Use a product such as Fray Check to help control raveling edges and stray threads. Just be sure to test first!

Paper will ruin your fabric scissors.

It is always helpful to keep two pair of scissors in your sewing area: one strictly for fabric, the other to cut "everything else." If, however, you discover that you have mistakenly cut a dozen paper templates with your precious Ginghers, don't panic! **The occasional use of fabric shears to cut lightweight paper (freezer, typing, or tracing paper) does not dull them any more than cutting fabric.**

Regular sharpening and oiling prolongs the life of your scissors and counteracts the dulling effects of both fabric *and* the occasional paper slipup.

Tip

Tie a strip of fabric to the handle of your best fabric shears. They'll be easy to distinguish at home and in a crowded classroom.

Quilt with a between, the "official" quilting needle.

While the between is designed specifically for quilting and is the needle of choice for most quilters, you may find this tiny needle hard to grip and manipulate. **If you have large fingers or difficulty due to minor arthritis (or another ailment) in your hands, try using a sharp.** A sharp is a little longer than the average between and makes a more than adequate substitute. Experiment to find a brand that feels comfortable; then progress to the smallest size you can handle, just as you would with a traditional between.

If a pattern is in print, it must be accurate.

As much as we wish this were true, we know that it is not always so! Even with the most *meticulous* editing, occasionally an error slips through to the finished book, magazine, or commercial pattern. **This is one reason most publishers recommend reading all instructions and making a test block before cutting all of the pieces for a quilt!**

If you discover a mistake in any printed pattern, by all means contact the publisher. Books and patterns can be corrected in a subsequent printing, or with a simple insert in existing copies. Magazines can note the change in a future issue.

Tip

It is *always* wise to make a test block before cutting an entire quilt. Variations in your cutting or seam allowances can affect block size.

QUILTING MYTHS LAID TO REST

A

Alternate block. A plain, pieced, or appliquéd block used to separate the basic blocks in the quilt.

Appliqué. Attaching small pieces of fabric to a larger background fabric by hand or machine stitching.

Appliqué stitch. Refers to an invisible hand stitch used to secure edges of appliqué shapes to the background. Also called a blind stitch.

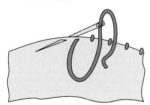

B

Background quilting. Repetitive motifs used in open areas of a quilt; they enable other designs to come forward to catch the viewer's eye.

Backing. The fabric that is used for the "wrong" side of a quilt to hold the batting layer in place. Quilt backings can be made from one piece of fabric or several lengths pieced together to be the appropriate size. Backings can also be pieced for a decorative look.

Basting. The process of temporarily securing the three layers of a quilt in preparation for quilting. Can be done using needle and thread, pins, basting gun, or basting spray adhesive.

Basting gun. A timesaving device that injects plastic tacks through all layers of a quilt to secure them for quilting.

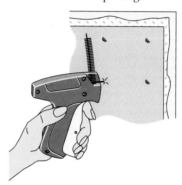

Batting. The invisible layer in a quilt. Usually made of cotton, polyester, or wool, batting is available in a variety of thicknesses. The fiber content of the batting dictates how close or far apart the quilt must be quilted to retain its shape, as well as how the finished quilt needs to be laundered.

Bearding. A fuzzy or "bearded" appearance that occurs when batting fibers work their way through the quilt top or backing. This condition happens primarily with polyester battings.

Beeswax. A waxy substance rubbed on thread to help stiffen and strengthen it, and to reduce tangles.

Betweens. Short, sturdy needles used for hand quilting. Betweens come in sizes ranging from 9 to 12. The rule of thumb is the larger the number, the shorter the needle.

Bias. The stretchy, diagonal grain of the fabric. True bias is at a 45 degree angle to the straight grain, but any off-grain cut may be referred to as a bias cut.

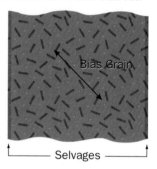

Bias Grain

Selvages

Bias binding. Any binding with edges cut along the bias grain of the fabric.

Bias press bars. Nylon or metal bars, available in a variety of widths. These bars are used to make accurate tubes from bias strips of fabric. After stitching a tube, the appropriate size bar is inserted into the tube before pressing. Finished bias tubes are used to create narrow elements that bend, such as vines, handles, stems, and tendrils. Also called Celtic bars.

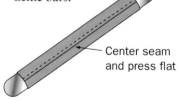

Center seam and press flat

Binding. A long, narrow strip of cloth that covers the raw edges of a quilt.

Binding clips. Barrettelike, metal clips that snap shut to secure the folded binding to the back of the quilt during final hand sewing.

Bleeding. Excess reactive dye that seeps from fibers when fabric is washed. The dye may stain other fabrics.

Block. One unit of a quilt top. A block may be pieced, appliquéd, or a combination of the two.

Blocking. Manipulating an irregular block while pressing in order to make it the exact size and shape it should be.

Butting seams. When aligning two patchwork units for stitching that already have seams in them, it is necessary to butt or nest the existing seam allowances together for a perfect seam intersection.

Chain piecing. An assembly line technique where pieces are paired together, then fed through the sewing machine one after another without lifting the presser foot or cutting the threads.

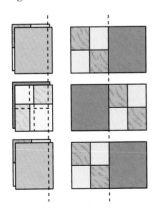

Cross-hatching. A grid of parallel quilting lines that form diamonds or squares. Cross-hatching may be done diagonally or on the straight grain.

Crosswise grain. The grain formed by the weft threads that run perpendicular to the selvages.

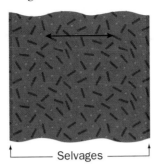

Selvages

Cutting mat. A protective mat made of self-healing material on which you can safely use a rotary cutter.

Darning foot. A presser foot with a large opening at its base. Used during free-motion quilting, this foot moves up and down with the needle, holding fabric in place when the needle is down, but allowing free motion of the piece when the needle is in the up position.

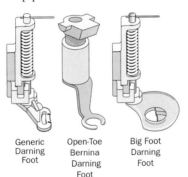

Generic Darning Foot   Open-Toe Bernina Darning Foot   Big Foot Darning Foot

Design wall. A place to position and shuffle quilt components during the design process. Often made of flannel or batting tacked to a flat wall or foam board.

Dimensional appliqué. Appliqué where the pieces are attached to the surface of the background fabric. Fabric may be folded, gathered, or stuffed to achieve a three-dimensional

look. Dimensional appliqué is especially popular in album-style quilts.

Directional print. Fabrics with distinct, one-way motifs, such as stripes.

Dog ears. Little triangles that stick out beyond the raw edge of a block or patchwork.

Trim off dog ears

Echo quilting. Concentric lines of quilting that produce repeating, or echoed, shapes. Echo quilting is most often used around appliqué shapes and quilted motifs. Rows of echo quilting can be spaced equally or by varying amounts.

Extension table. A work surface that fits flush with the throat plate of the sewing machine to support the quilt at one level and give you freedom to manipulate your quilt.

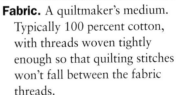

Fabric. A quiltmaker's medium. Typically 100 percent cotton, with threads woven tightly enough so that quilting stitches won't fall between the fabric threads.

Free-motion quilting. Sewing with the machine's feed dogs disengaged; it allows you to freely move the quilt under the needle, making stitches of any length and in any direction you choose. This type of quilting requires the use of a darning foot, which has a spring mechanism that allows it to bounce up and down on the fabric as the needle raises and lowers.

Freezer paper. A roll of household paper with one plastic-coated side. Its original purpose was for freezing foods, but quilters have carried it off to the sewing room for foundation piecing, template making, and appliqué.

Freezer paper appliqué. A variety of methods that use freezer paper as templates for pattern pieces. A freezer paper shape is pressed onto the fabric, where its plastic coating adheres it. Freezer paper can be used on top of the fabric as a guide to where to turn under the fabric edges, or it can be used on the bottom as a stabilizer when stitching the shape. Seam allowance edges are folded back onto the paper and glued, pressed, or basted in place.

Clip here

Freezer paper

Fusible web. A paper-backed adhesive product that allows you to permanently affix appliqué pieces directly to the background. Fusible interfacing, when used to face appliqués, is used in a similar manner.

Graph paper. Gridded paper that can be used as foundation material or to draft quilt blocks. It is also helpful in testing for a perfect ¼-inch seam allowance.

Hanging sleeve. A permanent or temporary tube of fabric on the quilt back that provides a place for inserting a dowel or other hanging device.

L

Label. A permanent or temporary message telling the history of the quilt and the name of the quiltmaker.

Latex gloves. Disposable "rubber" gloves used by medical professionals and anyone who wants to protect their skin while working. They are lightweight and flexible, so you can pick up pins while wearing them, yet their rubbery texture lets you grip fabric easily, so you can freely move your quilt under a darning foot while free-motion quilting.

Lengthwise grain. Created by warp threads that run parallel to the selvages in a piece of fabric. This grain direction is the most stable. It is virtually unstretchable.

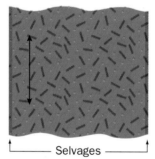

Selvages

Loft. The term used to describe the thickness of batting. Thicker, high-loft batts result in puffier quilts; thinner, low-loft ones yield flatter quilts.

Machine-guided quilting. Machine quilting done with the feed dogs engaged, such as stitch-in-the-ditch, grid quilting, and gentle curves. Also referred to as straight-line quilting.

Multiview lens. A lens that reflects multiple images of the object being viewed. Through it, one quilt block appears to be many identical blocks positioned side by side.

N

Needlepunching. A finishing technique used by manufacturers in which batting fibers are punched with special needles to bind them together. Needlepunched battings resist bearding. Both cotton and polyester battings can be needlepunched.

Needles. Sewing machine needles come in a variety of sizes and point styles, each suited to a different need. Sizes range from a very slim 65/9 to a large 100/16. Point styles are available in quilting, topstitching, embroidery, sharp, universal, jeans, and metallic.

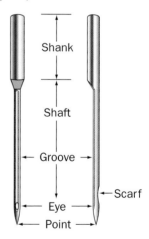

Shank

Shaft

Groove

Scarf

Eye

Point

Needleturn appliqué. A type of hand appliqué in which raw edges are turned under a very short distance at a time as pieces are sewn to the background. The tip of the needle is used to turn the seam under just before stitching.

O

Off-grain. A fabric that is printed so the pattern does not follow the straight grain, or a pattern piece that is not cut with the straight grain on at least one edge.

Outline quilting. Outlining a shape with a line of quilting stitches, often placed ¼ inch from the seam.

P

Patchwork. Small pieces of fabric sewn together to form a larger unit, quilt block, or quilt top.

Pin basting. Using safety pins, rather than a needle and thread, to hold the quilt layers together.

Pouncing. A marking technique in which a chalk-filled bag or other container is moved up and down on top of a stencil to transfer lines to fabric placed beneath it.

Pressing. Bringing the weight of an iron straight down on quilt pieces without moving the iron back and forth, in order to flatten seams without stretching or distorting the unit.

Q

Quilting hoop. A round or oval two-part "frame" that holds the layers of a quilt sandwich together and secure for hand stitching. A screw and bolt allow for tightening or loosening tension. The hoop is repositioned as you work.

Quilting in the ditch. Placing quilting stitches a needle's width away from a seam line to define a design in a quilt.

R

Reducing lens. A lens that reduces the size of objects being viewed, making them appear farther away. Ideal for viewing block settings and gauging their overall effect.

Rotary cutter. A razor sharp, rolling cutter that resembles a pizza cutter. A rotary cutter is used in conjunction with a special self-healing mat that protects the table surface and an acrylic ruler to cut fabric. For appliqué, it is helpful to have a square ruler (12½-inch or 15½-inch) for cutting background blocks accurately.

Rotary-cutting ruler. Also referred to as a see-through or acrylic ruler, this thick, rigid ruler allows quilters to measure fabric strips and hold them in place securely for rotary cutting.

S

Scrap quilt. A quilt made by mixing many different fabrics, rather than by repeating a few fabrics in identical blocks or units.

Selvage. Tightly woven, finished edges that run lengthwise along the fabric. They should be trimmed away and not used.

Silk pins. Long, very thin straight pins that glide through fabrics easily. These are the finest of straight pins. They leave virtually no holes in the fabric when they are removed.

Stencil. A quilting design cut out of plastic. Quilters can draw the quilting design onto a quilt top with a quilt marking pen or pencil by marking in each slotted opening of the channel-cut stencil.

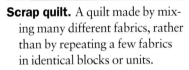

Stipple quilting. Very closely spaced, random lines that resemble pieces of a jigsaw puzzle; generally used to fill in small areas or flatten portions of a quilt in order to emphasize nearby raised motifs.

Straight grain. The lengthwise or crosswise threads in the weave of fabric.

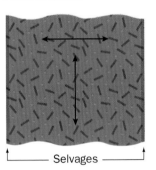

Selvages

T

Tracing Paper. Lightweight see-through paper that is available in art supply or department stores. It comes in sheets or on a roll. When placed over a design in a book, the lines are easily visible and can be copied to the tracing paper, then transferred to fabric or template material.

Quilter's
Marketplace

Check here for sources of hard-to-find or specialty items mentioned throughout the book. Also check with your favorite quilt shop to see if they carry specific items.

Adam Beadworks
P.O. Box 2476
Guerneville, CA 95446-2476
(707) 869-2556
Thread Heaven thread conditioner

Big Board Enterprises
P.O. Box 748
Hughesville, MD 20637
(800) 441-6581
Big Board

Block Party Studios, Inc.
922 L Ave.
Nevada, IA 50201
(800) 419-2812 or
(515) 382-3150
Fabrics, pens, preprinted labels, quilt tote bag, Quilter's Stuff bag, wheeled tote

Blue Feather Products, Inc.
165 Reiten Drive
P.O. Box 2
Ashland, OR 97520
(800) 472-2487 or
(541) 482-5268
Pin Place, Scissor Spot, Notions Nook, Grabbit magnetic pincushion

Clotilde, Inc.
B3000
Louisiana, MO 63353-3000
(800) 772-2891
Beam & Read Light (with AC adapter), Enlarger/Magnifier Light, Handeze gloves, Wrist-Eze band, Body-Rite, Magnifier Light, Beam and Read Light, MagEye, Zinger, rotary-cutter blade guards, portable ironing surfaces and boards, Thread Heaven thread conditioner, Roxanne's Glue-Baste-It, Sullivan's Basting Spray, June Tailor Grid Marker, general quilting supplies

Connecting Threads
P.O. Box 8940
Vancouver, WA 98668-8940
(800) 574-6454
Multiview lens, Tri-Sharp rotary-blade sharpener, general quilting supplies

Craftgard Company
P.O. Box 472
Tustin, CA 92781-0472
(888) 878-1212 or
(714) 730-3856
Craftgard, Quiltgard, Quiltwash, The Forever Box

Dreamworld Enterprises
6673 Main St.
Bonner's Ferry, ID 83805
(208) 267-7136
Sew Steady table

Keepsake Quilting
Route 25B, P.O. Box 1618
Centre Harbor, NH 03226-1618
(800) 865-9458
Fabrics and general quilting supplies

The Kirk Collection
1513 Military Ave.
Omaha, NE 68111-3924
(800) 398-2542
Antique and reproduction fabrics from 1850 to 1950; quilts, tops, and blocks; supplies for quilt-making; quilt conservation and restoration products

Nancy's Notions
333 Beichl Ave.
P.O. Box 683
Beaver Dam, WI 53916-0683
www.nancysnotions.com
Perfect Press and general quilting supplies

A Quilted Kitchen
9938 SW Terwilliger Blvd.
Portland, OR 97219-7701
(877) 516-0675
Clutter Gutter table

Quilts and Other Comforts
P.O. Box 2500
Louisiana, MO 63353
(800) 881-6624
Wire quilt hanger, quilting supplies, fabric

Sew-Ergo, Inc.
275 Waneka Pkwy., #6
Lafayette, CO 80026
(888) 739-8458 or
(303) 604-6101
Tilt'able and Sure Foot System

St. Peter Woolen Mill
101 W. Broadway
St. Peter, Minnesota 56082
(507) 931-3734
Nature's Comfort brown wool batting

The Summer House Needleworks
6375 Oley Turnpike Rd.
Oley, PA 19547
(610) 689-9075
Fabrics and block-of-the-month kits

T.J.'s Quick Quilter
13011 Chimney Oak
San Antonio, TX 78249
www.tjsquickquilter.com
T.J.'s Quick Quilter

The Thread Bare
Pattern Company
P.O. Box 1484
Havelock, NC 28532
(252) 447-4081
Ruler Roundup

Jane Hall and **Dixie Haywood** are award-winning quiltmakers who are known for adapting traditional designs using contemporary techniques and innovative approaches. Their quilts have been exhibited throughout the country and are in private and public collections. Both have been teaching and judging quiltmaking for more than 20 years and have a strong commitment to providing students with well-grounded and creative information so they can make their own unique quilts. They have coauthored *Perfect Pineapples, Precision Pieced Quilts Using the Foundation Method,* and *Firm Foundations.* Jane is a certified appraiser for old and new quilts. Dixie is the author of *Contemporary Crazy Quilt Project Book* and *Crazy Quilting with a Difference,* and her articles appear regularly in leading quilt periodicals. Longtime friends, Jane lives in Raleigh, North Carolina, with her husband, Bob; Dixie lives in Pensacola, Florida, with *her* husband, Bob. They rely heavily on the telephone, fax, and airlines to function as a team.

Cyndi Hershey has been quilting since 1978 and began teaching quilting in the early 1980s. Her background is in interior design and textiles. The colors, patterns, and textures of fabric are still the things that interest her most. Being able to combine so many different fabrics in one project is the primary reason that she loves quilting. She and her husband, Jim, bought the Country Quilt Shop in Montgomeryville, Pennsylvania, in 1988. Her favorite part of owning the shop is that it allows her to teach as often as possible, helping other quilters learn and grow.

Gail Kessler, former owner of The Summer House Needleworks quilt shop in Oley, Pennsylvania, is a well-known quiltmaking lecturer and instructor, specializing in hand quilting and appliqué. She combined her exquisite sense of color and design with keen business sense to create one of the most highly successful Block-of-the-Month programs in America. For more information on the more than 30 current offerings, or to receive the shop's Newsletter, see "Quilter's Marketplace" on page 124.

Nancy O'Bryant Puentes wrote the first book on caring for quilts in the home in 1986, after coordinating the nation's first quilt conservation and restoration seminar. Nancy is cofounder of the American International Quilt Association, the Alliance for American Quilts, and the Texas Sesquicentennial Quilt Association. She helped plan and direct the Texas Quilt Search and coauthored two books on historic Texas quilts.

Susan Stein has been quilting since 1977. She writes, teaches, and designs quilts for publications. She is the former owner of a contemporary quilt shop called Colorful Quilts & Textiles in St. Paul, Minnesota. She now lives in Delaware, Ohio, and shows her quilts in galleries throughout the state.

Janet Wickell has been quilting for many years, but it became a passion in 1989 when she discovered miniature quilts. For the past several years Janet has been a freelance writer and has contributed to many books for Rodale Press, including eight titles in the Classic American Quilt Collection series. She teaches quilting and hand-marbling fabric, and she also enjoys herb gardening, photography, and reproducing quilt patterns in stained glass. She is the author of *Quick Little Quilts.* Janet lives in the mountains of western North Carolina with her husband, daughter, and a growing menagerie of animal friends.

Darra Williamson is the author of *Sensational Scrap Quilts* and numerous magazine articles on the subject of quiltmaking. In 1989 she was named Quilt Teacher of the Year, and she travels extensively, teaching and lecturing at guilds and quilt events. She has served as a technical writer for various Rodale publications and is currently at work on a second book for the American Quilter's Society. In addition, she is an avid and knowledgeable baseball fan and maintains a notable collection of outrageous socks.

Experts Cited

Gloria Hansen, of Hightstown, New Jersey, an award winning quilter and coauthor of *The Quilter's Computer Companion.*

Nancy Kirk of the Kirk Collection. See "Quilter's Marketplace" on page 124 for further information on the Kirk Collection.

Sharon Hultgren, author, designer, and national teacher.

Tips from well-known quilters Mimi Dietrich, Sharyn Craig, Karen Kay Buckley, and Mary Stori.

Acknowledgments

Quiltmakers

We gratefully thank the following quiltmakers who graciously permitted us to show their projects as examples of the various tips and techniques described in this book:

Karen Kay Buckley, Caribbean Floral Fantasy on pages 103 and 105, Vegetable Garden on page 66, Flying Geese on page 34

June Culvey, Cardinal Virtues (backing) on page 112

Jane Hall, Los Ventos on page 103, Indigo on pages 4, 5, and 64, antique Amish quilt on pages 63 and 115, Etoile de Bordeaux on page 113, small silk pineapple on page 113, Chroma IV Canyon on page 65, Teleidoscope on page 64

Dixie Haywood, Amish Echoes #5 on pages 63, 64, and 115, Hospitality on page 65, Oak and Sumac on page 68, Remember Me on pages 90 and 96, Summertime on page 96

Becky Herdle, Robbing Peter to Pay Paul on page 115

Tanja Lipinski-Cole, Grandmother's African Flower Garden on page 104

Lytle Markham, dimensional appliqué block on page 76

Suzanne Nelson, Fantastic Sport Quilt on page 89, design/pattern by Four Corners Designs, (800) 573-3687; Cumberland Quilt on page 42, Aunt Sukey's Choice on page 80, antique quilt and Crown of Thorns on page 114

Ellen Pahl, Jake on page 61, from Alley Cats pattern from Red Wagon Originals, Linda Brannock, designer

Sally Schneider, antique quilt on pages 57 and 58

Karen Soltys, antique yo-yo quilt on page 65 and miniature log cabin quilt on page 66

Susan Stein, Sunrise, Sunset on pages 61 and 118, Petroglyphs on page 112

Mary Stori, Island Hopping and Cruise 1995 on pages 78 and 79

Darra Williamson, Star of the Bluegrass on page 54, Triangles on page 55, For Zachary on pages 65 and 109

Sample Makers

Sarah Dunn, Barb Eickmeier, Cyndi Hershey, Suzanne Nelson, Ellen Pahl, Susan Stein, Jane Townswick, and Darra Williamson

Fabrics and Supplies

Adam Beadworks—Thread Heaven thread conditioner
American & Efird—threads
Benartex—fabric
Bernina of America—sewing machine
Big Board Enterprises—Big Board, Mini Board, and covers
Blue Feather Products, Inc.—Pin Place, Scissor Spot, Grabbit Notions Nook, Grabbit Magnetic Pincushion
Block Party Studios, Inc.—fabrics, pens, labels, quilt tote bag, Quilters Stuff Bag, wheeled tote
Body Rite—back weight
Clotilde—Beam & Read light, magnifier light, Wrist-Eze band, and Hand-Eze gloves
The Country Quilt Shop—fabric, batting
Craftgard—Craftgard, Quiltgard, Quiltwash, The Forever Box
Dream World—Sew Steady tables
E.E. Schenck Company Maywood Studio—fabric
Emmaus Jewel Shop—pocket watch
Hoffman Fabrics—fabric

June Tailor—Cut 'n Press boards
J.T. Trading Corporation—505 Spray and Fix temporary adhesive
Mag Eyes—MagEyes magnifier
Olfa/O'Lipfa—rotary cutters and blades
Omnigrid—rotary-cutting mats and rulers
P & B Textiles—fabric
Patches country shop, Emmaus, PA—Boyds bears and row boat
Pfaff—sewing machine
Primrose Gradations—hand-dyed fabric
The Quilted Kitchen—Clutter Gutter table
Ready Bias—100 percent cotton quilter's binding
Robert Kaufman Co.—fabric
Rockland Industries—muslin
Rose & Hubble—fabric
Roxanne International—Roxanne's Glue-Baste-It
St. Peter Woolen Mill—brown wool batting
Sew-Ergo—Tilt'able and Sure Foot System
Sullivan's USA—Sullivan's basting spray
TRS Designs—Quilters' Companion Travel Organizer
Wrights—basting gun and basting tack remover
Yons Antiques, Limeport, PA—high chair

Index

INDEX

Quilting Styles

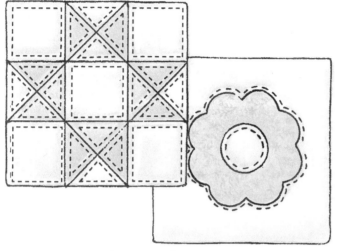

Outline Quilting

Echo Quilting

Single

Double

Crosshatch or Grid Quilting

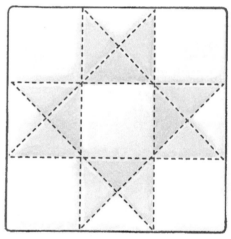

In the Ditch Quilting

Stipple Quilting

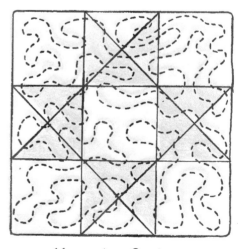

Meander Quilting